DESIGNING
Starts Here

. . . .

David M. Barlex ▪ *Nigel Read* ▪ *David Fair* ▪ *Carolyn Baker*

Designing Starts Here and the National Curriculum — 3

Introduction — 4

1 STUDENTS DESIGNING
Car games — 6
Body adornment — 10
Model movers — 14
Mechanical toys — 18
Kites and flyers — 22
Packaging — 24
Moisture sensor — 26
Windmills — 30
Shopfront design — 32
The challenge of survival — 34

2 YOU CAN DO IT TOO!
The untidy desk — 36
Looks good to eat — 37
Publicity and promotion — 39
Problems with play — 40
More about kites and flyers — 42

More about packaging — 44
Pop-ups — 46
Spinning games — 47
Music makers — 48
Puppet theatre — 49
More about survival — 50
More about wind energy — 52
More about shops — 54
Convenience food — 56
Carrying sports gear — 58
Warnings — 59

3 RESOURCES
Resources for Drawing and Modelling — 60
Resources for Understanding — 78
Resources for Action — 108

4 EVALUATING YOUR OWN WORK — 126

INDEX — 128

Hodder & Stoughton
LONDON SYDNEY AUCKLAND TORONTO

Acknowledgements

Barnabys Picture Library (18 right, 5 pictures; 34 bottom right; 51 bottom); Brighton Palace Pier (80 upper); Cabaret Mechanical Theatre (18 left, 3 pictures); The J Allan Cash Photolibrary (42 bottom); Department of Energy (85 bottom left, 2 pictures); Games Workshop 1990 – Advanced Heroquest the 3D Fantasy Roleplay Game (47); Leslie Garland (84 top left); Griffin and George (113); Intermediate Technology Development Group, Bob Harries Engineering Ltd (52); Mercury Educational Products (107 top); Meteorological Office, JFP Galvin (53); Nottingham Education Group (107 bottom right); Roddy Paine (9; 10, 5 pictures; 12; 13 left and right; 17; 20; 21; 25 top left and bottom right; 27, 4 pictures; 28; 29; 34 top left, bottom left, top right; 38; 39; 44; 45; 46; 49; 50, 3 pictures; 51 top; 54; 57, 2 pictures; 80 lower; 81; 82, 2 pictures; 83 top right and bottom; 84 bottom left, middle and top right; 86 bottom; 88; 90; 92; 94, 2 pictures; 95, 3 pictures; 98; 106, 2 pictures; 121, 5 pictures; 122); J Sainsbury plc (55); Science Photo Library (85 right, 2 pictures; 105, 2 pictures; 107 bottom left); Terry's Group (25 top left).

British Library Cataloguing in Publication Data

Designing starts here.
1. Design
I. Barlex, David M.
745.4

ISBN 0 340 49383 6

First published 1991

© 1990 David M. Barlex, Nigel Read, David Fair, Carolyn Baker

Typeset by Gecko Ltd, Bicester, Oxon
Printed in Hong Kong for the educational publishing division of Hodder and Stoughton Ltd, Mill Road, Dunton Green, Sevenoaks, Kent by Colorcraft Ltd.

DESIGNING STARTS HERE and the National Curriculum

No single book could hope to meet completely the challenge of Design and Technology (i.e. Profile Component 1 of the National Curriculum in Technology). *Designing Starts Here* provides a focus on the process of designing, in order to help students to become procedurally competent.

Designing Starts Here has been carefully structured so that it can be used flexibly in a variety of teaching and learning situations. Chapters 1 and 2 explore the process of designing through activities and examples. Chapter 3 provides a relevant knowledge base to which students are encouraged to refer, as appropriate, for information to develop their understanding of topics within the programmes of study. Chapter 4 deals with assessment.

Perhaps the most difficult aspect of designing is the need to retain an overview of the entire process while tackling the immediate details of stages within the whole task. Without this overview, students can lack a sense of direction. We have used a feature called the 'design strip' which will help to give this overview and confidence in tackling the individual but related elements within it.

The design strip is not a straight jacket to be slavishly and linearly followed. It is a guide to help students structure their design work.

The design strip relates to the N.C. Attainment Targets for Design and Technology as follows:

Attainment Target	1 Identifying needs and opportunities	2 Generating a design	3 Planning and Making	4 Evaluating
Design strip	The challenge Finding out	Thinking up ideas Developing ideas Modelling the best idea Presenting the best idea	Making it	Testing it

The spread of attainment levels likely among students at Key Stage 3 is from level 3 to 7. Whatever level a student is operating at, she or he should gain the confidence, understanding and skill to progress to higher levels. The design tasks in chapters 1 and 2 become more demanding towards the end of a chapter. This is reflected in the characters used. Ron, Lisa and Annabel are in year 7; Jon, Weng and Sharon are in year 8; Agnes, Darren and Julie are in year 9.

Designing Starts Here relates to the programmes of study for Key Stage 3 as follows:

Programme of Study	Developing and Using artefacts, systems and environments	Working with materials	Developing and communicating ideas	Satisfying needs and addressing opportunities
Designing Starts Here	Chapter 1 Chapter 2 Resources for Understanding	Chapter 1 Chapter 2 Resources for Action	Chapter 1 Chapter 2 Resources for Drawing and Modelling	Chapter 1 Chapter 2

INTRODUCTION

One of the most important features of our life today is that we spend most of our time in a 'made world'. All the things that we use have been designed and manufactured. Designing is so important that you need to know how to do it. The best way to find out about designing is to have a go yourself. We've broken the process of designing down into a set of parts which we call the design strip so that you can tackle the business of designing one step at a time.

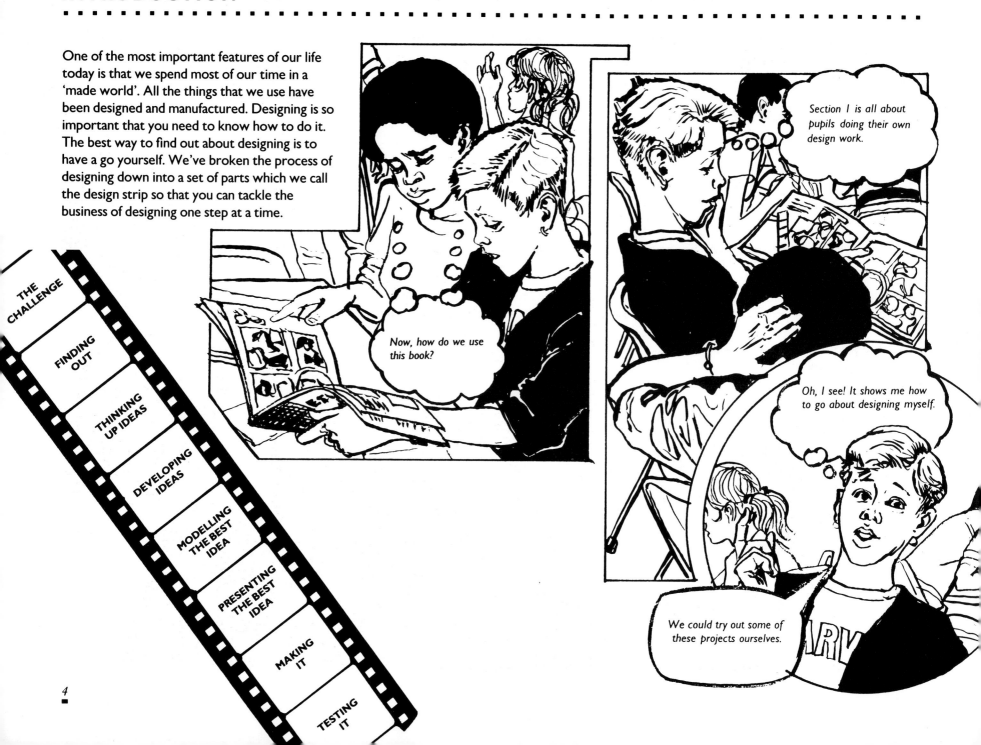

THE CHALLENGE

FINDING OUT

THINKING UP IDEAS

DEVELOPING IDEAS

MODELLING THE BEST IDEA

PRESENTING THE BEST IDEA

MAKING IT

TESTING IT

Now, how do we use this book?

Section 1 is all about pupils doing their own design work.

Oh, I see! It shows me how to go about designing myself.

We could try out some of these projects ourselves.

Car games

▶ THE CHALLENGE

It's all right for Ronabir, he can read, but Jit gets car sick if he so much as looks at a book.

He'll be more sick if he keeps saying how bored he is!

It's me who'll get into trouble in a minute for not amusing him. If only there was a game he could play. . .

▶ FINDING OUT

Ronabir decided to design a car game but he didn't know enough about them at first. He tried going to the library but he couldn't find anything really useful. So he decided to interview some of his brother's friends. This was easy as he could talk to them at the local playgroup. He realised that their parents might have important ideas but they were always very busy. He decided to produce a short questionnaire for them. To make it look professional, he used the school word processor.

Figure I *Producing the questionnaire*

Figure 2 *What does the customer want?*

Ronabir used the information that he collected to decide on the following important features of the game:

- it should be hand-held;
- it should be played by one player only;
- it should not be possible to lose or swallow any of the parts.

THINKING UP IDEAS

Ronabir wrote out a list of possible games and by using a table he compared them with the important features. He discarded any game that didn't have the key features. In this way Ronabir came up with a list of ideas that were worth developing further. His table is shown in Fig. 3. Ronabir's favourite idea was a maze game. He thought that this would be more fun than a steady-hand game and a lot easier to make than a mini bagatelle. He worked out that he could use a ball-bearing to follow the path of the maze. Now he had to develop a maze path which was challenging but not so difficult that it was impossible.

DEVELOPING IDEAS

Ronabir had to measure the ball-bearing accurately so that he would know the width of the maze track. He did this by seeing which hole in the drill box would fit the ball with a little room to spare. He found some string that was this thickness and used it to produce three different maze tracks on sheets of cardboard. He used these as formers to use for vacuum-forming

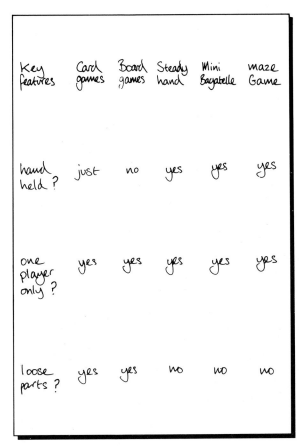

Key Features	Card games	Board games	Steady hand	Mini Bagatelle	Maze Game
hand held ?	just	no	yes	yes	yes
one player only ?	yes	yes	yes	yes	yes
loose parts ?	yes	yes	no	no	no

Figure 3 *Ronabir's table*

pieces of thin thermoplastic plastic sheet. He got his brother Jit to try out the three maze tracks and used the results to design and make a new maze track that was the right level of difficulty. Now that he had the maze track, Ronabir had to think about how to keep the track and ball visible without the ball getting lost. He decided to enclose the maze in a transparent plastic case. Some of his ideas for this are shown in Fig. 4.

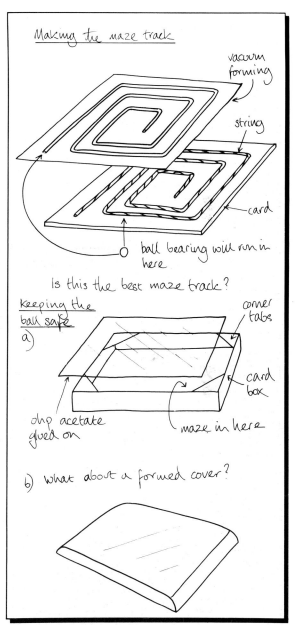

Figure 4 *Ronabir's ideas*

MODELLING THE BEST IDEA

Ronabir made a 3D mock-up in order to work out the details of his design. He made an overall shape from expanded polystyrene foam and used it to check the appearance and whether it was the right size for young children to handle easily. His first attempt, shown in Fig. 1, was too big so he adjusted the size of the maze to fit into a smaller shape.

Figure 1 *Using a model to check the size*

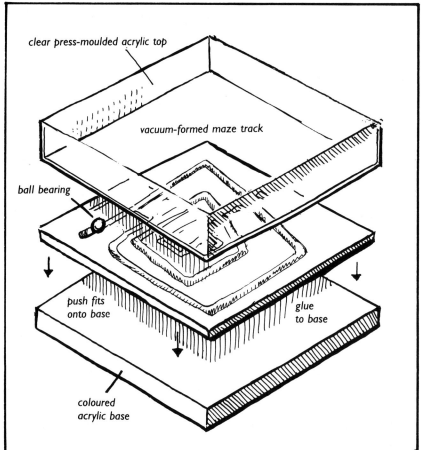

clear press-moulded acrylic top

vacuum-formed maze track

ball bearing

push fits onto base

glue to base

coloured acrylic base

Figure 2 *The parts of the maze game*

 PRESENTING THE BEST IDEA

To be sure that he had worked out the details needed to make his design Ronabir produced an exploded diagram showing all the parts, what they would be made from and how they would be made. This is shown in Fig. 2.

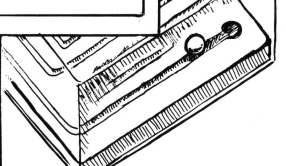

MAKING IT

Now that he knew what to make and how to make it, Ronabir had to decide the best order for making all the parts. He drew the following flow chart.

1. Make former to press-form lid

2. Press-form lid. Trim and polish edges

3. Mark out and cut base from acrylic sheet. Polish edges and check that it will fit tightly into lid.

4. Vacuum-form the maze insert using redesigned former.

5. Trim to size that fits exactly onto base leaving no gaps between insert and lid.

6. Glue maze insert onto base.

7. Put ball bearing into maze and push-fit cover onto base.

Figure 3 *The finished game*

TESTING IT

Ronabir was pleased with his maze game but wanted to be sure that it really would keep young children amused. He decided to visit the playgroup and watch while several children 'had a go'. He thought it would be worth trying to answer these questions.

- Did they like its appearance?
- Did they find it easy to use?
- Did they find it fun to play with?
- Did it stand up to their use without breaking?

The most interesting thing he found out was that the game worked best when the player had someone watching. The players could take it in turns to see who could do it more quickly.

ACTIVITIES

1 Lots of games are advertised to make them attractive to potential customers and so to increase sales. Develop some ideas for advertisements that would make Ronabir's game seem a worthwhile purchase to parents of young children.

2 People are often bored when travelling in trains and coaches, as well as in cars. The game Ronabir designed is only suitable for young children. Develop design ideas for travelling games that might appeal to older children, teenagers and adults. The games should include some of the following features:

- easy to use while travelling;
- entertaining;
- original idea;
- if not original then an existing game presented in a new way.

Resource Links ▷

Use the Electricity and Electronics Resource section to help you answer the following questions.

1 Design an adjustable timer that would sound a 'time's up' warning.

2 Design a circuit that would give an indication (such as a light coming on) of when the maze game is successfully completed.

3 What changes would you have to make to Ronabir's design to include these features?

Body adornment

THE CHALLENGE

Lisa was given a challenge by her D and T teacher. She had to design and make an item of personal adornment that was attractive to look at and practical enough to wear comfortably.

The project was an introduction to using wood, metal and plastic in a decorative way, so the design had to use a combination of these materials. The main materials available were:

- 5 mm thick hardwood;
- 5 mm thick acrylic;
- 1 mm thick aluminium sheet.

Lisa's teacher asked the class to do some finding out before the next lesson. The following tasks were set:

Homework - Monday Sept 8/Technology
1. Look for pictures of people in traditional costume from different countries around the world.
2. Look for close-up pictures of people from historic times.
3. Look for pictures of people dressed in an unusual fashion.
Make a record of anything interesting in your folder.

... I'll go and have a look in the library when I go into town on Saturday...

FINDING OUT

Lisa found plenty of pictures to get ideas from. You can see below how she presented them in her folder. She cut these ideas out from old magazines.

My brother's got that book on cowboys and Indians. I could draw the Red Indian head-dresses...

THINKING UP IDEAS

In D and T the following week the teacher asked the group to draw ten different designs, using the pictures they had collected for homework as a starting point. Beside each drawing they had to note which materials they would use and how the item would be worn. Here are some of Lisa's first ideas.

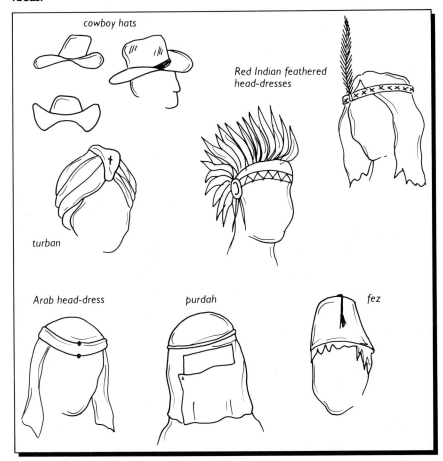

cowboy hats

Red Indian feathered head-dresses

turban

Arab head-dress

purdah

fez

Figure 1 *Lisa's first ideas*

ACTIVITIES

Lisa was able to think of several different and interesting ideas using shapes and patterns from the pictures she found. Can you think of some more? Set out your ideas clearly on plain paper.

DEVELOPING IDEAS

Lisa decided that she liked the cowboy theme. She developed her ideas on this by producing a series of drawings of the hat and head until she had one which looked right and was easy to make. She did this by deliberately using only straight lines because shapes made by straight lines are easier to cut out than curves. Her sketches are shown in Fig. 2. Note that it took her several attempts to get the proportions just right.

She also produced a set of additional designs on the cowboy theme based on the equipment that cowboys use. She thought that if she finished her main design quickly then she could try these too.

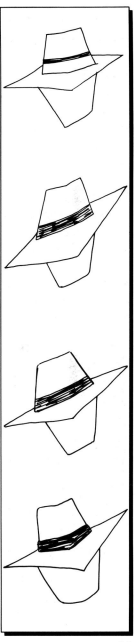

Figure 2 *Lisa's design developed through careful drawing*

MODELLING THE BEST IDEA

To be sure that the design would work, Lisa made two models. The first was from card and kitchen foil. First she cut out the complete shape from plain card. Then she cut out the hat shape from brown card and the face shape from pink card. She stuck them onto the base card and added a thin strip of kitchen foil for the hat band. She was not happy with the way the card fitted together and decided to make a plasticine mock-up to give the model the same thickness as the materials she would use in her final design. As she mounted pieces of coloured plasticine onto a card base, she realised that she would have to file the plastic and the wood very carefully to get the precise fit needed.

PRESENTING THE BEST IDEA

To be sure that she had all the details of her design worked out, Lisa produced a set of full-size card templates. She thought she would be able to use the card templates for marking out and then for checking that each piece had been finished to just the right size. She also drew a clear exploded diagram showing how all the parts, including the pin, fitted together.

Figure 1 *The models Lisa needed to make to check out her design*

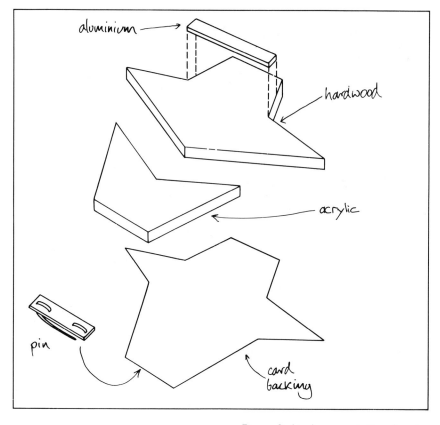

Figure 2 *Lisa's presentation drawing*

MAKING IT

Lisa used the card templates to mark out the pieces. By positioning the templates carefully on the material she avoided waste and minimised the number of cuts she had to make. As she was cutting straight lines she used a junior hack-saw for the acrylic and a tenon-saw for the hardwood. She cut the aluminium sheet using tin snips. She used flat files and abrasive papers to remove the marks left by the sawing. She finished off the acrylic edges and the aluminium strip with metal polish. She protected the hardwood piece with polyurethane varnish. When she was satisfied with the appearance of the pieces and the way they fitted together, she stuck them onto the cardboard backing piece with Araldite. She asked her teacher to help her stick the aluminium strip onto the acrylic with superglue. Finally she stuck the brooch pin she had bought onto the back with Araldite.

TESTING IT

Lisa tested her new brooch by wearing it for the first time at a friend's birthday party. She didn't tell anyone that she had made it but just wore it and waited to see if anyone noticed or commented on it.

Lisa wondered if she could sell brooches like this so she visited a local craft stall and showed it to the owner. The owner liked it but suggested that the card backing piece should be made from thin plastic sheet. She said that she could probably sell them for £2.00 each and would take 30p commission on each one sold. This would leave Lisa with £1.70 for each brooch, less what she paid for materials, consumables and fixings. The brooch took Lisa nearly three hours to make. Is Lisa likely to earn a lot of money by making jewellery like this? How could she increase her profits?

Figure 4
Lisa's brooch

Figure 3 *The materials and tools Lisa used to make her brooch*

Figure 5
Is it worth it?

Model movers

▶ THE CHALLENGE

Annabel's young cousin, Adrian, was coming to stay with her as part of a birthday treat. She wanted to make him a present and knew that Adrian had lots of toy people. He was very keen on space and hospitals and he would bring these toys with him.

I know! I'll make him a toy person transporter that can move.

Figure I *Adrian likes playing with toy people*

Annabel's challenge was to design and make a toy person transporter that was battery-powered and which could be controlled.

▶ FINDING OUT

Before she started designing, there was a lot to find out. Annabel had to know the sizes of the ring cans, motor and battery (from which she would make the transporter). This was easy because she knew how to measure. She collected pictures of ambulances from newspapers and magazines. She found pictures of space vehicles in science fiction comics. She stuck all of these in her design scrapbook. Annabel also checked that she had the sorts of material and parts she would need: wooden strip for a chassis, paper and card for a body, old ring cans for wheels, knitting needles for axles, plus rubber bands, paper fasteners, drawing pins, a 9 V battery and connector, and an electric motor.

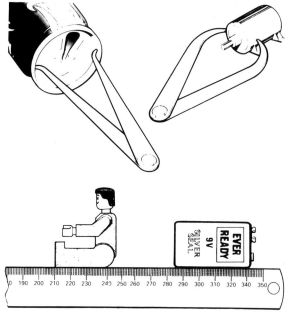

Figure 2 *Measuring accurately is important*

ACTIVITIES

In your workshop, use the instruments shown to measure the items that Annabel needed. Present your results alongside a sketch of each item. Make sure the measurements are in millimetres.

Resource Links ▷

Annabel needed to find out how to make the motor turn the wheels. Use the Mechanisms section to find out about belt drives. She also wanted the toy to go backwards and forwards. Use the Electronics section to find out how to make a reversing switch.

THINKING UP IDEAS

Annabel drew a flow chart to help her explore possible shapes for the toy. She used this to decide on a modern ambulance shape. She used a similar chart to work out how the toy people were to go in and out.

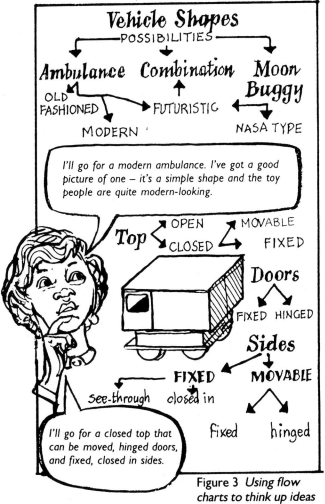

I'll go for a modern ambulance. I've got a good picture of one – it's a simple shape and the toy people are quite modern-looking.

I'll go for a closed top that can be moved, hinged doors, and fixed, closed in sides.

Figure 3 *Using flow charts to think up ideas*

Figure 4 *One idea for a space transporter*

ACTIVITIES

Use flow charts to think up shapes for a transporter carrying people in space.

DEVELOPING IDEAS

To develop her ideas further, Annabel drew plan and side views of the chassis showing clearly where the axles, cans and motor would go and how it would all be held together. By adding a side view of the body she saw that she needed a floor above the cans for the toys to stand on. She was also able to check that there was enough room for the toys to stand up without their heads touching the roof.

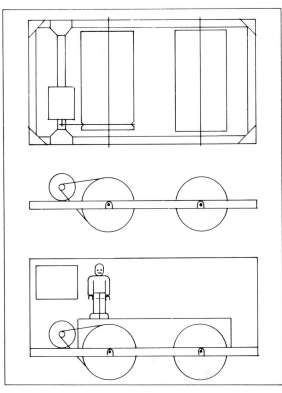

Figure 5 *These drawings helped Annabel develop her ideas*

ACTIVITIES

1 Annabel's plans are not complete. What further details are needed before she can make her design? Present your answer as a list.
2 Making a body shell of paper is a quick way to explore the shape of something. Try some of the following: another vehicle, a block of flats, a church, a tortoise.

Figure 1 *Using a paper mock-up to ensure a good fit*

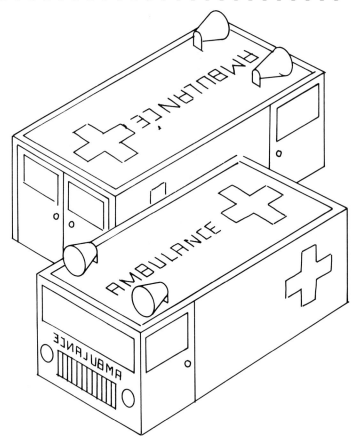

Figure 2 *Drawing the real thing helps get the details right*

MODELLING THE BEST IDEA

Annabel learned a lot from her simple model. She needed to work out ways to join the floor to the rest of the body shell. She also realised that the final body shell would have to be made very accurately if it was to fit the chassis. It would also need reinforcement if it was to stand up to a child's use.

PRESENTING THE BEST IDEA

Annabel did two sorts of drawing to get the detail of the design just right. The first was a full-size plan and side view of the chassis. She used this to check the lengths of wooden strip and positions of holes. The second was a pictorial drawing of the ambulance on which she noted all the realistic details to be added to the toy.

MAKING IT

Now that Annabel had complete plans for her design she had to work out the best way to make it. She decided on the following order.

a *Assemble the chassis with the ring can wheels.* She cut the side pieces to size and drilled the axle holes in both pieces at the same time. Was this a good idea? She fitted the axles into the frame before gluing it together with the card corners. Why?

b *Fit the motor, belt drive and control leads.* She found the motor had to be in just the right place for the belt drive to work. She found this by making the position adjustable. Can you work out how to do this?

c *Assemble and fit the card body shell.* She drew the network and added the lettering and details *before* assembly. Why?

TESTING IT

Annabel decided that she would look at these features:

- movement;
- controlling the movement;
- appearance;
- how well it carried the toy figures;
- robustness (strength);
- how much Adrian liked it.

ACTIVITIES

1 Annabel found that the toy people fell over when the toy moved. What can you design to solve this?

2 The corners of the card body shell soon became dented. Annabel did not have the time or money to use a more robust material. What else could she do?

3 Adrian said that he liked the toy. How can Annabel be sure he wasn't just being polite?

Resource Links ▷

1 Annabel found that the toy moved too quickly. Use the Mechanisms section to find out about ways of reducing speed.
2 Annabel was not happy with the quality of the lettering. Use the Drawing and Modelling section to find ways of improving this.

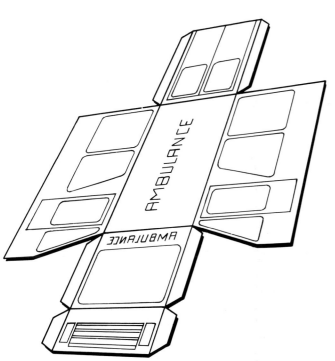

Figure 3 *The body shell before assembly*

Figure 4 *The toy transporter finished*

Mechanical toys

▶ THE CHALLENGE

Jon went to a craft shop when he visited London and saw lots of mechanical toys. Some were very large and complicated, others were small and worked very simply. The ones he liked the most were those that looked like animals. They all cost more than he could afford so he decided to make one for himself. When he got home from the trip and began to think about this, he realised that he didn't know enough about the shapes of animals or the way they moved.

Figure 1 *Mechanical toys – attractive and intriguing but expensive to buy*

Figure 2 *Jon's animal scrapbook*

▶ FINDING OUT

Jon went to the newsagent and bought some wildlife magazines. He cut out pictures of the animals that interested him and stuck them in a scrapbook. He wrote down which parts he would like to be moving in a toy model of each animal. For a lion he thought it would be a good idea for the head to lift up as though the lion was roaring. Perhaps the tail could move as well? For a macaw he thought the beak could peck at a nut that was held in a claw and the claw could move up to the beak. Jon was particularly keen on the crocodile. He thought the jaws could open wide and snap shut, and the tail move from side to side. He found the close-up pictures of crocodiles' eyes quite frightening and thought it would be good to make the eyes look fierce. The pictures in his scrapbook did not show him how the animals moved, so Jon decided to keep any arms and legs on his toy still. This left plenty of other parts to move.

THINKING UP IDEAS

Jon decided to concentrate on the crocodile. Most of the toys he had seen put the working parts in a box beneath the moving figure. He thought this was a good idea as it would let him get at the mechanism easily. His first step was to decide on the input motion. Was this to be by a motor or by someone turning a handle? As he had enjoyed turning the handles on the toys in London, he chose this. So the input was slow rotary motion. He chose two output motions – the mouth would open and close and the tail would move from side to side. Both the mouth and the tail had to be pivoted so that they could move. This led Jon to think of the crocodile in three parts – the main body and lower jaw, the upper jaw, and the tail. He also realised that the mouth movement (up and down) was in a different plane to the tail movement (side to side). He sketched the three parts and how they were to move – these are shown in Fig. 3.

DEVELOPING IDEAS

Now he was clear about the input and output movements, he needed to work out ways of making the input cause the output. Jon couldn't make gears or afford to buy them so he ruled them out. He could use a cam to push a freely-moving rod to raise and lower the upper jaw. The cam could be mounted on a drive shaft turned by a handle. The rod would move up and down through a hole in the lower jaw. Jon had seen tails which moved from side to side by means of a peg on a wheel fitting into a slot in the tail. The problem with this was that the wheel and peg rotated at right angles to the drive shaft. How could he drive the mechanism to move the tail with the drive shaft? The simplest way to turn the drive through 90° was by using a friction drive between two wheels at right angles. Jon sketched these ideas (they are in Fig. 3). They looked as though they would work but he was not completely sure of details like the shape of the cam or the exact length of the slot in the tail. He needed to make a working model.

Figure 3 *Movements and mechanisms for Jon's crocodile*

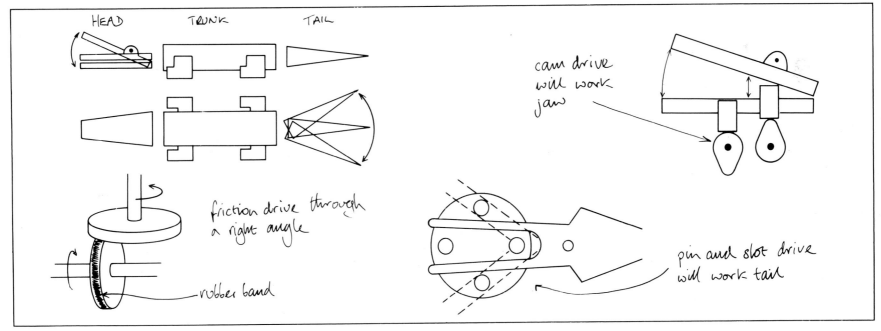

MODELLING THE BEST IDEA

Jon began his modelling by doing some accurate drawing. He drew a full-size side view of the crocodile's head with the upper jaw in both the open and closed positions. From this he worked out where the jaw pivoted and how far the rod had to move to open the mouth. Once he knew this he could design the cam to move the rod. He did this by adding a 'bump' to a circle as shown in Fig. 1. Jon drew a plan view of the tail with the tail in three positions – central and at both of the limits of its swing. He used the plan to work out how far the peg moving the tail had to move, and from this the length of the slot in the tail. To check that these really worked he made the models shown in Fig. 2 using stiff card, softboard and drawing pins.

Figure 2 *Checking the mechanisms by modelling*

PRESENTING THE BEST IDEA

By modelling through drawing and card mock-ups, Jon was able to build up a clear picture of all the details of his design. From these he drew a complete picture (Fig. 3) which showed all the things he needed to know in order to make the toy work. In separate diagrams he drew complete plans for the framework holding the mechanism and supporting the crocodile, and details of the curtains to let people see the workings. He also drew the shapes of all the crocodile parts, noted the colour scheme and listed all the materials he would need.

Figure 1 *Analysing the movements by drawing*

Figure 3 *Jon's drawing has all the information he needs to make the crocodile work*

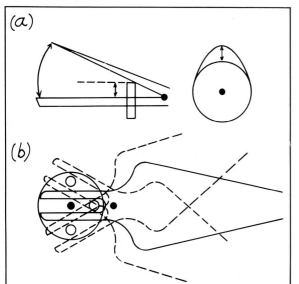

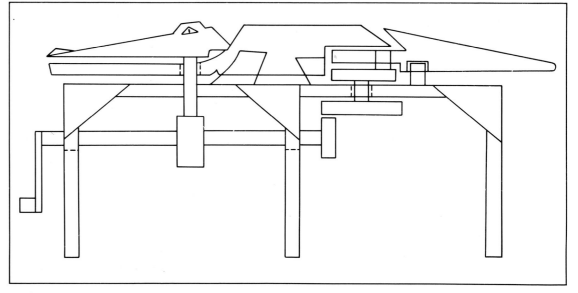

1. Mark out sides and top of frame.
2. Cut out and drill.
3. Assemble frame.
4. Mark out parts of crocodile.
5. Cut out and shape.
6. Match up with hole in top and drill hole in lower jaw.
7. Stick legs to body.
8. Mark out cams and wheels.
9. Cut out and drill.
10. Cut wooden pin and fit to wheel.
11. Cut drive axles to length.
12. Push fit cams and wheel onto main drive axle and position in frame.
13. Push fit tail drive and assemble in position in frame.
14. Locate tail on fixed pivot over tail drive mechanism, ch that it works.
15. Place body/lower jaw in position on frame and attach upper jaw with Sellotape. Ch position and working.
16. Remove crocodile part and paint.
17. Mark out and cut turni handle parts.
18. Push fit handle onto drive axle.
19. Cut out and hem curt
20. Sew on curtain ring
21. Add screw eyes a wire to frame.
22. Put up curtains.
23. Position crocodile frame and locate (a)
24. Attach by gluing feet to top.
25. Attach movable jaw by fabric hinge.

Figure 4 *Doing things in the right order is half the battle*

MAKING IT

Now Jon had to find the best way to make his design. To do this he worked out a flow chart which listed what he had to do and the best order to do it. You can see part of it in Fig. 4. There were several stages where accuracy was important. For example, aligning the holes for the drive shaft in the end plates, and drilling the axle holes on the cam and drive wheels. Jon's methods for achieving the required accuracy are shown in Fig. 5. Jon was particularly pleased with his method for decorating the crocodile. He covered the parts with a layer of polyfilla and scratched it to give a texture that looked like crocodile skin.

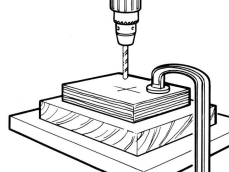

Using centre finder for marking centres on drive wheels

(a)

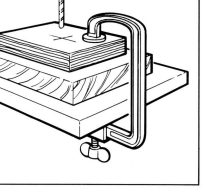

Drilling shaft holes in end plates at the same time

(b)

Figure 5 *Ways to ensure accuracy*

Figure 6 *Jon's crocodile*

TESTING IT

Jon used the following questions to help him test his toy.

- Do the tail and mouth move when I turn the handle?
- Does the animal look like a crocodile?
- Are any of the parts easily breakable?
- Will any of the parts wear out quickly?

ACTIVITIES

Resource Links

Use the Electronics and Mechanisms Resources sections to help you.

1 The jaws open and the tail wags for every complete turn of the handle. How can you make this happen once every five turns?
2 Work out a way to use red LEDs in the eyes to light up when the mouth opens.

Kites and flyers

▤ FINDING OUT

When Weng saw people flying kites in the local park, he thought he'd like to try it for himself. He wanted to make one but wasn't sure how to begin. He started by going to the reference library and making some notes about different sorts of kites, how to make them and the history of kite flying. He talked to his mum who told him about a specialist kite shop in the next town. When he visited the shop he found that it stocked a whole range of materials and fixings specially for kite making, as well as ready-made kites. From his research, and after talking to the shop assistant, he found that there were seven types of kite – flat, bowed, box, sled, parafoil, compound and delta. His sketches and notes are shown in Fig. 2.

Figure 1 *Flying kites looked like fun*

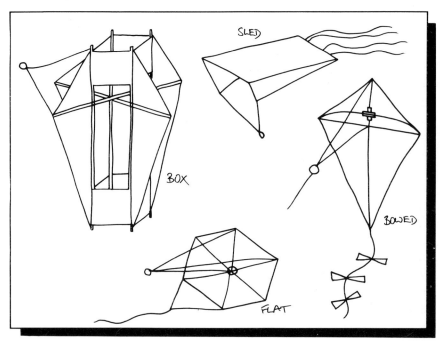

Figure 2 *Weng's sketches of different kite shapes*

Fabric	strength	wet strength	weight	colours	cost
Tissue paper	very low	very low	very low	many	low
Crepe paper	low	very low	low	many	low
Polythene	fair	good	low	few	low
Cotton sheet	fair	good	heavy	many	moderate
Canvas	high	good	very heavy	many	high
Tyvek	very high	very good	low	white	very high
Tear-resistant nylon	very high	very good	low	many	very high

Figure 3 *Weng's chart comparing materials*

Weng soon realised that most kites consist of a framework covered with a fabric. The material for the framework must be stiff, strong and light. The fabric must be light and tear-resistant. He found that there were several materials that met these requirements and his choice would depend on how much he could afford as well as the sort of kite he wanted to make. His charts comparing materials are shown in Fig. 3.

Weng decided to make both a flat kite and a bowed kite. His design sketches are shown in Fig. 4. He found that different sorts of kite need different wind conditions to fly at their best. He produced a chart which showed how to tell what the conditions were just by 'looking', and which kites were best for which conditions. This chart is shown in Fig. 5.

Figure 4 Weng's first design sketches

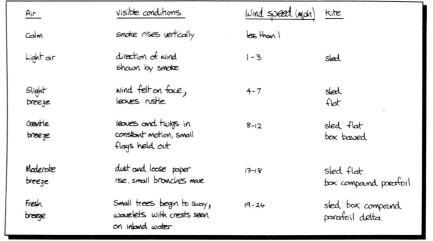

Figure 5 *Weng's notes on flying conditions*

Air	visible conditions	Wind speed (mph)	kite
Calm	smoke rises vertically	less than 1	
Light air	direction of wind shown by smoke	1-3	sled
Slight breeze	wind felt on face, leaves rustle	4-7	sled flat
Gentle breeze	leaves and twigs in constant motion, small flags held out	8-12	sled flat box bowed
Moderate breeze	dust and loose paper rise, small branches move	13-18	sled flat box compound parafoil
Fresh breeze	Small trees begin to sway, wavelets with crests seen on inland water	19-24	sled box compound parafoil delta.

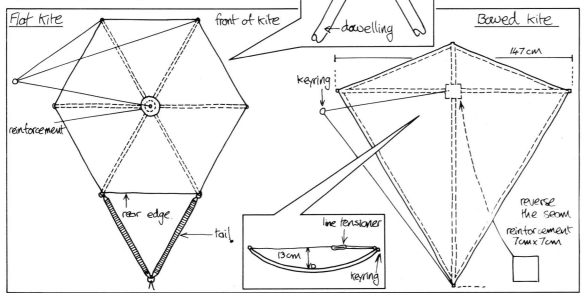

ACTIVITIES

1 Devise a series of tests to find out which of the following fabrics is best for kites: cling film, tissue paper, polythene sheet (dustbin bag), cotton sheet, crepe paper. You will need to test wet strength, dry strength, ease of gluing, and ease of stitching.

2 Many kites from the Far East are beautifully decorated. They often have fierce faces because they were used in religious festivals to ward off evil spirits. Design a series of kite 'faces'. You can choose a different emotion for each face: sad, happy, fierce, frightened. Remember to keep the design simple so that it can be recognised from a distance.

3 Try making a bow kite using Weng's design. You will find it needs a tail for stable flying. Experiment with different designs of tail until you find one that works. You will need to consider the weight and the length of the tail as well as the overall appearance.

Packaging

Hey! Look at this!

MODELLING THE BEST IDEA

Ronabir took the container home. He was surprised at how complicated it was. There was only one piece of card but it had been cut and creased so that it folded into a 3D container. There were only two places where glue was needed, (see Fig. 1). Ronabir collected other card packets to see if they were made from only one piece of card too. Pyramint and Toblerone packets are shown in Fig. 2. Each has only one glue tab.

ACTIVITIES

1 Collect several small cardboard sweet packets and carefully open them out. Present them as a display with notes to explain how they can be assembled into a packet, paying special attention to creases, tuck-in flaps and glue tabs.

2 Collect a large cardboard sweet packet (Easter egg boxes are ideal) and carefully open it out. You will find that it uses more than a single piece of card and sometimes involves vacuum-formed packaging. Present the pieces as a display with notes to explain what each does and how they can be assembled.

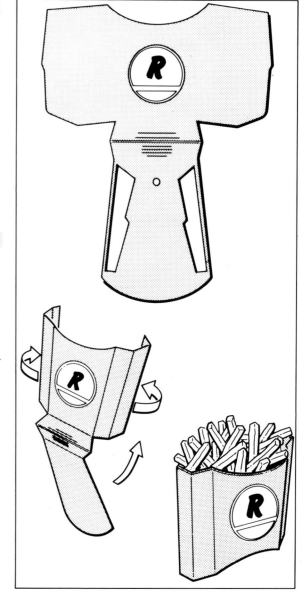

Figure 1 *The container holds the produce and advertises the producer*

Figure 2 *Modern sweet packaging*

Resource Links ▷

Ronabir decided to package the maze game he had made for his brother. He knew the size and shape of the game so he tried to design some nets that could be folded up to produce an attractive box. His best idea featured a see-through window and is shown in Fig. 3. To be sure that this would give the effect he wanted he made a full-scale mock-up, complete with colour and graphics. He was a bit disappointed with the overall effect (shown in Fig. 4) because it looked dull.

1 Use Resources for Drawing and Modelling to help you improve Ronabir's design. Explain clearly how the changes you have made improve the packaging.
2 Produce a model of your improved version.

Figure 3 *Ronabir's packaging idea*

Figure 4
Ronabir's model

Moisture sensor

THE CHALLENGE

Oh no, not again!

Mum, my plants keep dying.

Try watering them.

I keep forgetting.

I need some way of testing the soil for water...

FINDING OUT

Agnes started by visiting the local garden centre to find out how much water different sorts of indoor plant need. She was surprised to learn that some need watering several times a week while others can go for months without watering. She also found that plant pots come in a wide range of sizes but are usually made from clay or plastic.

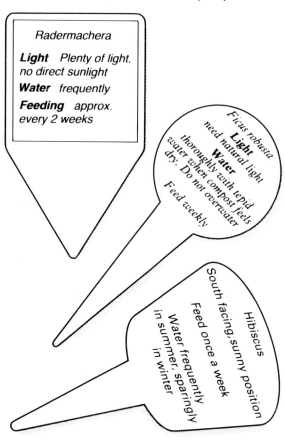

Radermachera

Light Plenty of light, no direct sunlight
Water frequently
Feeding approx. every 2 weeks

Ficus robusta
Light need natural light
Water water thoroughly with tepid water when compost feels dry. Do not overwater
Feed weekly

Hibiscus
South facing, sunny position
Feed once a week
Water frequently in summer, sparingly in winter

Figure 1 *Different plants need different conditions*

Figure 2 *Different pots and different soils*

Agnes then looked at how soil changes when it dries out. She found that it gets more crumbly and lighter in colour as it dries. She knew from her science lessons that the water in soil contains lots of dissolved solids and conducts electricity, although not very well.

THINKING UP IDEAS

From her research, Agnes thought she had the following options for the way her moisture detector might work.

a A system that weighed the pot plus plant plus soil and gave a warning below a certain weight.
b A system that could detect colour changes in the soil and gave a warning when a 'dry' colour appeared.
c A system which monitored the conductivity of the soil and gave a warning when the soil became dry.

Agnes rejected (a) because the system would need adjusting for different sized pots and because the only weighing machines she had seen looked very complicated. She rejected (b) because she had no idea how to detect colour changes other than by looking at the soil and she already knew that she forgot to do this. So she was left with (c). She had to find a way to measure the conductivity of the water in soil.

DEVELOPING IDEAS

Agnes decided to model circuits that might work. To begin with she tried to use the simple circuit shown in Fig. 3a to show that water in soil conducts electricity. She found that the bulb didn't light up when the probes were put in tap water. She tried the same experiment using an LED (light-emitting diode) and it did light (Fig. 3b). Then Agnes realised that she wanted a circuit that gave a signal when the soil was dry,

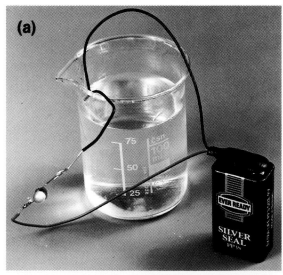

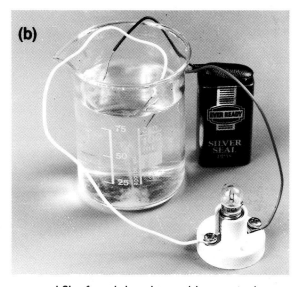

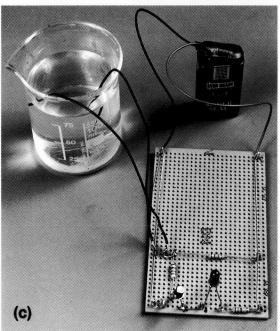

Figure 3 *The three circuits that Agnes tried out*

not wet! She found that she could use a single transistor circuit to light an LED when the probes were taken out of water (Fig. 3c). As she wanted the circuit to take up as little room as possible, she decided to use a printed circuit board (pcb) as shown in Fig. 4.

Figure 4 *Agnes made a printed circuit board to hold the components*

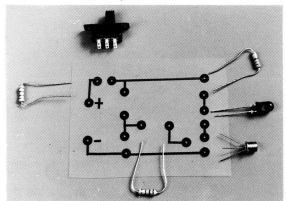

MODELLING THE BEST IDEA

Now that she had a circuit which worked, Agnes had to build this into a finished product. To do this she had to ask these six questions.

- What overall size is practical?
- Given this size, where will the battery fit?
- Where will the on/off switch go?

- How can I protect the circuit?
- How can I make sure that the LED is clearly visible?
- What do I want the finished product to look like?

Agnes worked out the answers to these questions by making a series of cardboard and balsa wood models. When she finished she had all the details worked out.

PRESENTING THE BEST IDEA

Agnes decided to combine the probes and circuit onto a single pcb and to cover the battery and circuit with a vacuum-formed polystyrene cover that was screwed onto the circuit board. The battery was held in place with double-sided tape and both the on/off switch and the LED stuck through the cover. Her presentation drawing plus notes are shown in Fig. 2.

The balsa wood models helped me to get the overall size and shape right. The card models helped me to see how to fit everything inside.

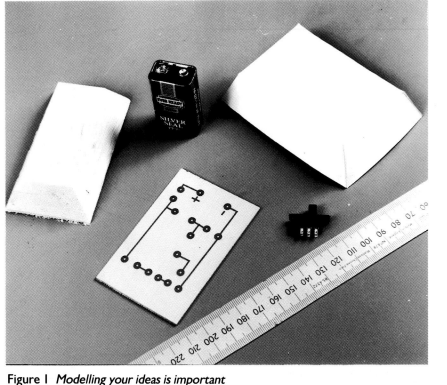

Figure 1 *Modelling your ideas is important*

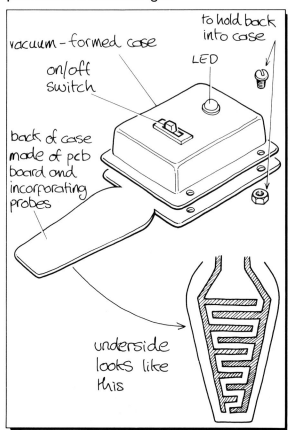

Figure 2 *Agnes' presentation drawing*

MAKING IT

Agnes then wrote a flow chart describing the order for making her moisture sensor:

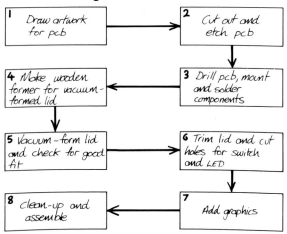

1 Draw artwork for pcb	**2** Cut out and etch pcb
4 Make wooden former for vacuum-formed lid	**3** Drill pcb, mount and solder components
5 Vacuum-form lid and check for good fit	**6** Trim lid and cut holes for switch and LED
8 Clean-up and assemble	**7** Add graphics

Agnes did the making in this order and found she had to alter her wooden former in order to get a good fit on the pcb.

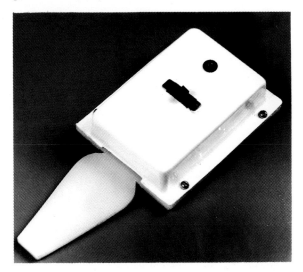

Figure 3 *The finished moisture sensor*

Agnes showed the sensor to her mum. Here's what happened.

Look Mum. Here it is, and it works.

Well it looks good, but does it work?

When the red light comes on I know I have to water the plant.

It all depends on whether you notice the red light then.

Do you think Agnes' mum is right?

TESTING IT

Agnes tested her moisture sensor by trying it out in four types of soil: very wet, damp, almost dry, and totally dried out. She found that the LED lit up with the dry and almost dry, but not with the damp or very wet. Should she be satisfied with these tests or should she try soils with a water content between damp and almost dry?

ACTIVITIES

1 How easy will it be to change the battery? Can you think of a better way to hold the battery in place?
2 Do you like the appearance of Agnes' moisture sensor? Can you improve it?

Resource Links ▷

Agnes thought the screws looked out of place. Can you think of a better way to hold the cover in place? Use the Assembling Section of Resources for Action to help you.

Windmills

TESTING IT

Julie became interested in wind energy after seeing a windmill. She wanted to build a small windmill to charge car batteries. She visited the library and made notes. On the right is a page from her notebook.

Type 1
Flat bladed
Horizontal Axis
Blades angled
to the wind

Must face into the wind

Type 2
Savonius
Rotor

Catches wind from ANY direction

Julie decided to base her design on type 1 because she thought this would be simplest. Here is her design:

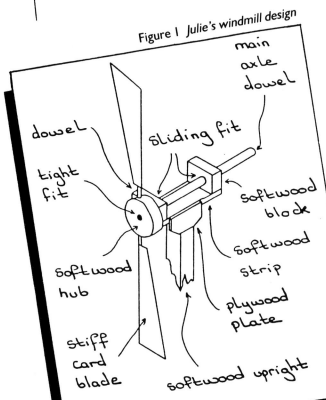

Figure 1 Julie's windmill design

main axle dowel

sliding fit

dowel

tight fit

softwood block

softwood strip

softwood hub

plywood plate

stiff card blade

softwood upright

I wasn't completely sure about the details so I decided to build a small model so that I could check. I made the model adjustable so that I could experiment to get the best performance

What shape will be best? narrow at hub, wide at edge wide narrow

narrow   **wide**   **wide at edge**   **narrow at hub**

How many blades will be best? Can I design hubs to take different numbers of blades?

What angle to the wind should the blade be?

angle of blade can be adjusted by twisting

TESTING IT

By testing the model (using a vacuum cleaner to provide the wind) Julie was left with three possibilities for the best arrangement. She had to test the performance more accurately. She did this by comparing how long the different arrangements took to lift a 100 g mass through a metre.

I used the Energy section on page 84 to find out how to work out the power of the best arrangement.

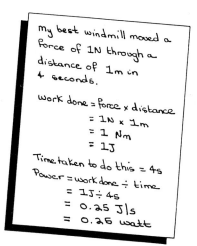

my best windmill moved a force of 1N through a distance of 1m in 4 seconds.

Work done = force × distance
= 1N × 1m
= 1 Nm
= 1J

Time taken to do this = 4s
Power = work done ÷ time
= 1J ÷ 4s
= 0.25 J/s
= 0.25 watt

Figure 3 *Julie's power calculation*

Figure 2 *Julie's windmill ready for testing*

1 m

100 g

ACTIVITIES

Will Julie be able to make her design? Use the Resources for Action section to help you answer the following questions.

1 How would you make the circular hub?
2 How would you mark it out so that it could take 2, 3, or 6 spokes and an axle?
3 How would you drill the hub to take the axles and spokes?
4 How would you fix the bearing blocks to the crosspiece?
5 How would you attach the blade to the spokes?
6 How would you finish your design to protect it from the "outdoor" environment?

Resource Links ▷

1 Julie chose mainly wood for her design. Use the Materials section to find out what else she could have used for:
the blades, the hub and the bearing blocks.

Use the Energy section to help you answer the following questions.
2 How much work has been done by these other windmills made in Julie's class?
Caldip's lifted 2 N through 1 m;
Jane's lifted 5 N through 2 m;
Craig's lifted 0.2 kg through 0.5 m.
3 How much power do these other windmills made in Julie's class have?
Mary's lifted 0.1 kg through 1 m in 5 seconds;
John's lifted 0.5 kg through 1 m in 1 second;
Leroy's lifted 5 N through 0.5 m in 2 seconds.
4 How long will it take the most powerful of these windmills to lift 4 N through 4 m?
How else might Julie test her windmill?
5 Draw a diagram to show how she might connect it to a dynamo and light a bulb. What measurements will she need to make to measure the power?

Shopfront design

DEVELOPING IDEAS

Darren usually walked to school every morning. It wasn't far and the journey was quite interesting as he passed several different shops. When he compared them he was surprised at how different each one was even though they all had the same basic structure – a large display window and a door. Each shopfront had its own style which was in keeping with the products it sold. There was one exception, a very run-down general store. It sold foods and drinks, sweets, cigarettes, stationery, newspapers, magazines, a small amount of domestic hardware, cheap toys and clothes. The windows were dirty, the display was hardly ever changed; inside the shop was poorly lit and badly organised. Darren wondered how the shopkeeper managed to make a living. One day he had a look inside and decided that the shop could be improved with some good organisation and a change of image. He decided to tackle it as a D and T project.

Figure 1 *The baker's*

Figure 2 *The off-licence*

Figure 3 *The greengrocer's*

Figure 4 *Yuck!*

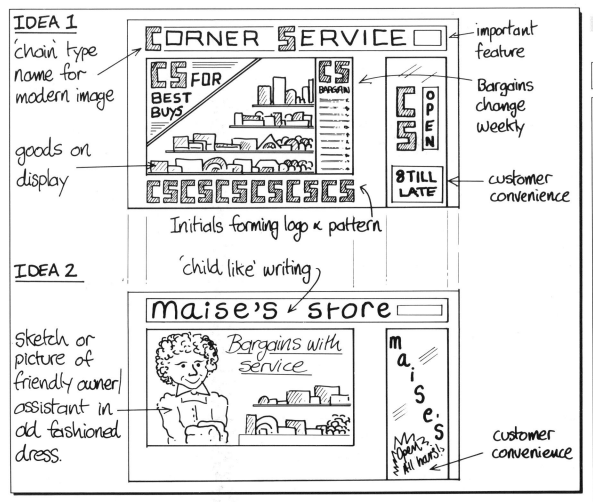

IDEA 1
'chain' type name for modern image

goods on display

important feature

Bargains change weekly

customer convenience

Initials forming logo & pattern

'child like' writing

IDEA 2

sketch or picture of friendly owner/assistant in old fashioned dress.

customer convenience

Figure 5 *Darren's ideas for a modern corner shop*

Darren began by drawing several copies of the shopfront and sketching in different ways of organising it to attract customers into the shop. Two of his ideas are shown in Fig. 5. He tried hard to give the impression of the shop being as well organised as a supermarket, but still keeping the personal service of a corner shop. He spent a long time thinking about the name and a logo. In the end he dropped the idea of a logo because these were usually only used by large organisations and this made them unfriendly. Do you think he was right?

Resource Links ▷

Use Thinking It Through and Showing Others of Drawing and Modelling to help you with the following activities.

1 Continue Darren's designing and develop several more sketches of a corner shop that has a shopfront in keeping with both a modern image and personal service. You will need to pay special attention to the use of colour, lettering and logos.
2 Turn the best of your ideas into a stand-up model of the shopfront. Make sure you include some cut-out figures in order to give a sense of the real size.
3 Make additions to your model by designing the interior to go behind the shopfront.
You will need to develop a way of displaying all the different types of goods that are sold. Some will need special storage facilities like a freezer or cool cabinet. Remember also that, in addition to being well-organised and providing friendly service, the goods must be arranged in a way that is convenient for the shopkeeper and which deters shoplifting.
4 If time permits, turn your designs for the interior into a 3D model to go behind the shopfront.

Figure 1 *Canoeing is fun*

The challenge of survival

The students in Year 9 were going on an adventure holiday as part of their social and personal development course. They knew that they would be in dangerous situations and they were asked to think about what precautions to take and what to do if things went wrong.

For canoeing, it was obvious to all of them that wearing life jackets was a sensible precaution. Climbing was another activity. This worried Darren as he suffered from vertigo (fear of heights). His teacher said that he could overcome this and that he would always be 'tied on' so that he could not hurt himself seriously. Going for walks across wild and windy places was also on the agenda. Waterproof and windproof clothing was especially important here because it can be dangerous to get very cold when you are in isolated areas.

As the students were to be out all day, they had to decide what food and drink to take and how to carry it. If they were overtaken by the weather and had to stay out overnight, a simple packed lunch would not be very substantial!

Figure 2 *You need a head for heights to do this!*

Figure 3 *You need warm clothes for orienteering*

Figure 4 *Hot food is always welcome*

As part of their preparation for the holiday Agnes and Julie decided to work out an emergency 'overnight in the open' survival kit. They began by making a list of all the things they thought they would need. They came up with the following list:

food and drink,
materials and tools to build a simple shelter,
sources of heat and light,
cooking and eating utensils,
first aid materials,
and signalling equipment.

They discussed this with their PE teacher who was very keen on outdoor pursuits and who had a mountain leadership certificate. She thought that they had covered most of the basics but suggested a map and compass as well. They then turned this general list into a detailed one and considered how all the items could be packed safely into a rucksack. In the end they decided to design a special container for the supplies and equipment. This had to be lightweight and hold the contents in a way that gave easy access. Their choice of contents is shown in Fig. 5. Have they missed anything vital?

ACTIVITIES

1 Using the materials and equipment that Julie and Agnes chose, or your own choice, explore ways to pack everything into a container. You will need to find out the shapes and sizes of all the items before you begin. They may be organised in a variety of ways – all on one level, on two or more levels, according to use, according to size, it's up to you. Whatever order you decide on it is

Figure 5 *Have they missed anything vital?*

important that you give your reasons.

2 Darren decided that he would make a container to hold the items in the way that Julie and Agnes wanted them organised. Use thin card to make a mock-up of the internal details of a container that fits the way you want the items arranged.

3 Julie and Agnes chose to include heavy duty polythene and light alloy tubing to build a shelter. They had not worked out exactly how this would fit together. They thought they might be able to use Velcro fastenings to make the shelter draught-proof. Using paper and straw, make some models to work out the details.

4 Agnes was interested in the possibility of including some easy-to-read instructions in the kit. Produce a small booklet that will help anyone to use the contents of the emergency kit to their best advantage. Keep the writing to a minimum and use lots of diagrams.

Resource Links

Use the Shapes and Sizes section to find out about the space that a body needs in a variety of positions. This will be useful when deciding on the size of the polythene needed for the shelter. Use this section also to find out about the spaces into which people can easily get their fingers.

Use the Materials section to identify materials that could be used for the container and organising partitions. Whatever is chosen will need to be easily shaped, lightweight, strong, stiff and unlikely to corrode or rot.

The untidy desk

Annabel begins to face the problem of her desk by asking some questions.

- How much desk top do I have? How wide? How long?
- What do I keep on the desk top? Do I need all these different things?
- Which things do I use a lot?
- Which things do I use only sometimes?
- Which things do I hardly use?
- What sizes are the different things I keep on the desk? Can I put them in groups of similar shapes? Long and thin, short and thin, squarish?
- What about the tiny things like paperclips and drawing pins?
- Where are the best positions to keep the things that I use? How will they fit into the space available on the desk top?

These questions helped Annabel to gather the information she needed to design and make containers to keep her desk tidy.

She decided that the best way to handle all this information was to put it in a table. Can you design a table that will hold all the necessary information?

ACTIVITIES

If you have an untidy desk problem try using Annabel's question list to help you design and make the answer.

Many designers have tried to solve this problem and different sorts of desk tidies are on sale in most stationers. Check them out to see if they really do hold everything you are likely to need.

If you have a hobby – electronics, cosmetics, painting, model making, hairdressing, computing – you may find it difficult to store all you need in tidy but easy-to-get-at ways. Use Annabel's question list, and any extra questions that your particular hobby makes necessary, to solve your storage problem.

Whatever you make should look good and be in keeping with the surroundings. You will need to decide about the style and appearance of the containers you design.

Resource Links ▷

These Resource sections will help you meet 'untidy' challenges:
Drawing and Modelling to explore style, page 63–65, 70;
hand sizes, page 79;
choosing materials, page 80;
joining materials, page 114;
vacuum-forming for display trays, page 113.

Looks good to eat

ACTIVITIES

1 Collect the wrappers and packets from a variety of 'ready-to-eat bars' – sweets, biscuits, snacks etc. Mount each one on a card and note down which features make it attractive and eye-catching. Try to decide what it is that each wrapping says about the product that will make it appeal to the people who buy it.

2 Many of the wrappers you have collected will be for products that are advertised on television. Look carefully at one or two of the advertisements and ask yourself what the advert is saying about the product. For example: it will make you more healthy, you can eat it without getting fat, it's full of 'goodness', people of a particular type eat it while they're having a good time. Can you see how the advertiser is trying to say to a particular group of people, 'if you buy this product, you'll be getting what you want out of life'?

3 Carry out a survey of 'health food' bars available in your local shops and compare the contents of each. The best way to present your results is to use a series of bar charts. Is there any relation between price and content?

4 Design a questionnaire to find out what sort of foodstuffs people want in a health food snack bar. Use this information to design a healthy snack bar that contains no more than 5 pence worth of foodstuff.

5 Design the packaging to go with your health food snack bar. How will you make it attractive to those people who like 'healthy' food? Make mock-ups of your most successful designs.

Lisa and Ronabir are excited about 'The Carrots' pop group's first live gig in the local Community Centre. Lisa's older brother is the guitarist and Ronabir's older sister is the vocalist.

The local Community Centre

This is so embarrassing – there's hardly anyone here!

I feel sorry for them. They've worked hard for this.

The next day at Lisa's home

Last night was disastrous! I think we'll have to call it a day.

You need better publicity – that's all. These posters aren't exactly inspiring!

What about a new name – 'The Carrots' sounds so stupid!

COME TO THE CARROTS

We've been doing logograms in D and T at school. If the band had a logo it could be shown on posters and stickers. We could even make badges!

Yes, a lot of famous pop groups have a logo which you see on their records and on T-shirts, posters and calendars. It's all part of their image.

Figure 1 *Pop posters*

Publicity and promotion

Any event like a carnival, marathon run, flower show or pop concert, which relies on a large attendance for its success, must be publicised. The publicity also depends on how much money is available; advertising can be costly when it involves printing, and radio or television adverts can be very expensive. Publicity also depends on the type of people that the promoters want to attract and how many people will be needed to make the event successful.

Lisa and Ronabir are determined to make The Carrots' second gig more successful than the first by attracting more people. They need to answer these questions.

- How should they go about promoting it – publicity, badges, T-shirts, hats?
- What type of people should they attract? How will this affect the promotion?
- What type of publicity is most appropriate – posters, handouts, a spot on local radio?
- Where should they display posters and sell tickets?

Figure 2 *Pop 'promo' products*

ACTIVITIES

Resource Links

Use Showing Others in Drawing and Modelling to help you tackle these activities.

1 Develop a new name and logo for 'The Carrots'.
2 List a range of products that could be used to promote the pop group and show by means of sketches how the logo and new name may be incorporated into them.
3 Produce a poster to advertise the next gig. The layout will be important. The poster will need to be laid out in a way that reflects the new image. You will need to work out a style of lettering that fits in with the group's new name and logo. It is important that the poster is attractive both from a distance, so that casual observers will take a further look, and close up, so that information about the gig is easy to read.
4 Design a ticket for entrance to the gig with a counterfoil that could also be used for a prize draw.

Figure 1 *Heck! Wait till Mum sees this*

Figure 3 *Trouble – any minute now*

Problems with play

You will almost certainly have had problems in finding suitable places to play. Indoors at home is often difficult because there's not enough room, things get broken and you can't make a mess. Playing in the street solves some of these problems but gives rise to others. If you make lots of noise you annoy the neighbours and they complain to your mum and dad. It's easy to break windows as well, and there is always the danger of traffic. Waste ground a short distance from your home (away from neighbours) seems like a good idea at first but it also has several drawbacks. There's often quite a lot of rubbish there. Some of it is good for building hide-outs but some is dangerous and dirty. There is always the possibility of undesirable strangers hanging about on waste ground. Parks offer wide open spaces so they are good for chasing about, playing ball games, throwing things and flying kites; but sometimes parks can be a bit boring if they are just open spaces.

Figure 2 *Easy to see how kids get hurt*

Figure 4 *But there's nothing to do!*

PLAYGROUND DESIGN

Designers have produced playgrounds to solve the play problem. However, nearly all playgrounds have been designed by adults. Here's a chance to design your own. The problem facing you is that children will want excitement and this usually means danger. Your design will have to balance safety against excitement. You can divide play equipment into two sorts.

a *Play Structures.*
Children can climb, crawl and wriggle in these while pretending to be in an adventure – lost in an underground world, escaping from a dungeon, defending a castle. It is the imagination of the child that provides most of the excitement but being up high or hidden away will add to this.
b *Rides.*
These include swings, roundabouts, slides and rocking horses. It is the movement that provides excitement, sometimes coupled with being up high.

ACTIVITIES

1 Find out about your local playgrounds by visiting them. If there is a play structure, make a detailed sketch and decide whether it is a good stimulus for children's imagination. Decide also whether it is safe, giving reasons for your decision. You will need to consider the surface beneath the structure. Why?
2 Develop a design for a play structure to be used by children aged 7 to 14 by making a small-scale model using card, sticks and string.

Figure 5 *Exciting rides – but are they safe?*

Try to make sure that your design is better than any play structure in your area.
3 Find out how the length of a swing chain affects the time of a swing by building a simple scale model. Try to estimate the safest height for a swing.
4 Develop a design for the best shape and height for a slide by making simple models.
5 Use modelling to help you solve the problems below.

- Passers-by are sometimes hit by swings.
- Children sometimes fall out of swings.
- Children sometimes fall down the steps leading up to a slide.

Resource Links

1 Use the Shapes and Sizes section to find out how high children of ages 7 and 14 can reach. Why is this information important in designing a play structure?
2 Use the Structures section to see if you can imagine the forces in the play structures shown in Fig. 5.
3 Use the Materials section to find out which materials could be used to make outdoor play structures and how they might need to be protected.
4 Use the Energy section to help you identify the energy changes taking place in children using swings and slides.

More about kites and flyers

TRADITIONAL KITES

Kites were first developed in the Far East almost 4000 years ago. They were used in religious festivals to attract the attention of evil spirits. In addition to being given interesting shapes like fish, dragons and other imaginary monsters, they were fitted with whistles and clappers which made noises in the wind.

It was very important that the spirits did not ignore the kites. Those kites with a 3D framework sometimes carried candles so they became flying lanterns. At the height of the ceremony, the kite strings would be cut and the spirits would follow the kites as they moved up and away with the wind, leaving the people below free from their evil intentions.

Fig. 1 shows an example of an Oriental paper kite. The designer managed to produce the most striking decorations without interfering with the flying performance of the kite.

Figure 1 *An Oriental paper kite*

Figure 2 *Sky-diver in dihedral form*

MODERN KITES

Traditional kites are flat and need a tail for stability. The dihedral kite shown in Fig. 3 does not need a tail as its V-shaped wing prevents spinning and wobbling. The sky-diver shown in Fig. 2 uses the same idea to control his flight. He spreads his arms and legs to form a dihedral.

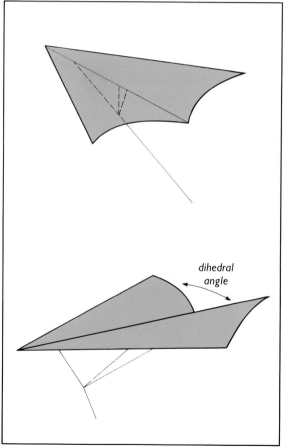

dihedral angle

Figure 3 *Dihedral kite*

ACTIVITIES

Construct a dihedral and a flat kite and compare their flying performance. Try to answer the following questions for both light and strong breezes.

- Which is the easiest to launch?
- Which gains height the fastest?
- Which flies the highest?
- Which is the most stable?
- Which is the easiest to control?
- What adjustments can you make to improve the flying performance?

HOT AIR BALLOONS

Hot air balloons were the first form of air travel. In 1783 a balloon made from paper and linen carried two men over Paris. Hot air balloons rise because the hot air inside them weighs less than the same volume of cold air. Once the air inside cools down then they sink back to earth. The early hot air balloons burned wool and straw to keep the air inside the balloon hot. Modern balloons are made from tear-resistant nylon and carry cylinders of propane gas to heat the air, but they work on exactly the same principle as the early balloons.

ACTIVITIES

You can use the information in Fig. 4 to help you design and make your own hot air balloon. Use the shapes shown in Fig. 4 to make card templates for panels that can be joined together to form a range of balloon shapes. You will need to scale up the template so that your balloon is a reasonable size.

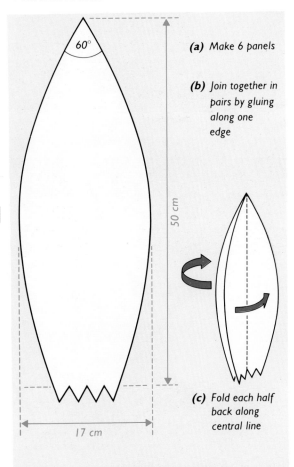

(a) Make 6 panels

(b) Join together in pairs by gluing along one edge

(c) Fold each half back along central line

(d) Now join pairs together to form a balloon

(e) Use the triangular tabs to hold a circle of thin wire to the base of the balloon

Figure 4 *How to make a hot air balloon*

You can use different materials to make the panels: polythene sheet, tissue paper, tracing paper, tear-resistant nylon. You will need to ask yourself the following questions before deciding.

- What's available?
- How much does it cost?
- Can I stick it together?
- What range of colours are there?

You can fill your balloon with hot air by using a fan heater or a Bunsen burner. You must be very careful not to set fire to the balloon.

Once you have made a set of panels and joined them into a balloon shape you can investigate how well your balloon performs for each of the following.

Flight duration – time taken from point of release to the contact with the ground.
Hover time – how long your balloon stays at a constant height in the air.
Stability – does the balloon wobble, lean to one side or turn upside down?
Height achieved – how high does it fly; how can you measure this?
Carrying capacity – how much extra weight will it lift?
Speed of ascent – time taken for your balloon to reach its maximum height.

If you work with others and test several different balloons you should be able to compare your results and use them to find out what is needed for good performance. You will then be able to redesign your hot air balloon for improved performance. Your new design should also try to make the balloon look as impressive as possible.

More about packaging

Gone are the days when most things were bought in a brown paper bag. It is easy to dismiss packaging as unimportant because it is usually thrown away when the contents are unwrapped. However, packaging is extremely important. It is used for several purposes:

- to protect the contents from damage;
- to make them easy to carry;
- to make them safe to carry;
- to make awkwardly-shaped objects easy to stack;
- to make the product look attractive;
- to make the brand of the product instantly recognisable;
- to hold lots of small items easily;
- to give the product an appropriate status;
- to allow bar coding.

Whenever a manufacturer launches a new product, or range of products, a lot of time is spent designing the packaging because this will play a large part in whether the product sells. People will only buy a new product if they are attracted to it in the first place and it is usually the packaging that they see first. If that does not get their attention then they don't buy it. Of course, it is not just the packaging that is used to attract the buyer. Advertising plays a large part as well. The advertising has to present the product as it will appear in the shops so most advertising features the packaging as well as the product. Sometimes manufacturers deliberately change

Figure 1 *Packaging products*

the packaging without changing the contents. This is usually linked to an advertising campaign that sells the product on the grounds that it hasn't changed – as good as always – but is now somehow better because of its new packaging – easier to carry or easier to recognise. Surely people aren't that gullible? They are! Manufacturers spend millions of pounds each year ensuring that their products continue to sell. Repackaging is standard practice.

Many products are packaged in shell structures made from cardboard. Recently, small items have been packaged in blister packs. This allows the item to be displayed so customers can see what they are buying. This packaging usually consists of a backing card with the article enclosed in a vacuum-formed or blow-moulded clear plastic bubble. The design of the backing card is very important as it carries all the additional information required to attract customers. Many blister packs are designed so that they can hang on display racks.

Many types of packaging are linked to a particular lifestyle. The packaging (and the advertising) might say 'here is a product used by people who are young and up-to-date'. Or they might say 'here is a product that is used by people who

Figure 3 *What do you see, the product or the pack?*

value the traditional and don't like new-fangled gadgets'. The product could be the same tin opener in both cases. The packaging has been carefully designed to appeal to different consumer groups.

ACTIVITIES

1 Collect a range of product packages (and if possible details of TV advertising) and for each one try to identify the consumer group that the producer is trying to attract. Are the potential customers seen as old or young, married or single, male or female, modern or traditional, ordinary working people or upper class? Try to work out as much as you can about the lifestyle and values of the target group.

2 Collect some of the advertising that banks and building societies produce to attract young people to open current accounts. Look at it critically and try to work out how the advertising tries to appeal to young people. Compare it with advertising literature aimed at attracting older customers.

3 Design the packaging for a range of cosmetics designed to appeal to teenagers, both boys and girls. You may need to find out what is already on the market. If time permits, produce high-quality mock-ups with a distinct image and brand identity.

Figure 2 *Blister pack*

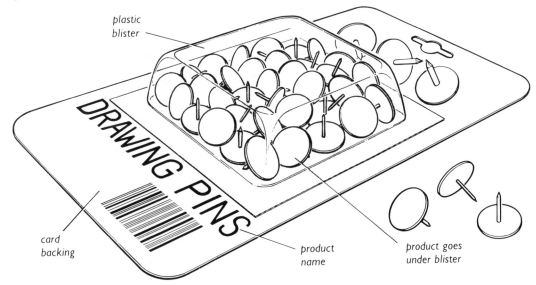

plastic blister

card backing

product name

product goes under blister

DRAWING PINS

Pop-ups

Weng was given a pop-up birthday card and was fascinated by how it worked. He thought that he'd like to have a go at making one. When his best friend had to stay off school for a few weeks through illness, Weng decided to design a pop-up 'get well' card to cheer him up. Weng had to think about what to put on the card and which part would pop up. He looked at some pop-up cards in a shop and discovered that most of them use the same type of folds.

Figure 1 *Pop-ups*

multiple layer pop-up card *V-shaped card*

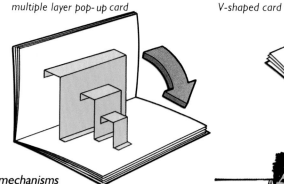

Figure 2 *Pop-up mechanisms*

Weng's finished card opened out to reveal a cartoon of his friend in bed looking poorly. The bed looks three-dimensional because it is part of the pop-up feature. So are the words 'Get well soon'. Weng made several paper mock-ups to start with, to get the right sizes and positions for the pop-up parts. This was harder than he thought it would be. One problem he had to solve was how to position the pop-up parts so that they wouldn't overlap the edges of the card when it was closed. The tabs also needed careful positioning. Weng discovered that they had to be stuck down parallel with the edges of the card, otherwise they wouldn't fold properly when he tried to close the card.

ACTIVITIES

1 Using the pop-up constructions shown in Figs. 1 and 2 as a starting point, design a pop-up greeting for someone you know. Remember to model your ideas in paper first. Use stiff paper or thin card to make your best ideas.
2 Once you have mastered the basic pop-up folds try some more adventurous designs,

My mate thought this card was great!

So did my teacher.

He's set our class a pop-up project!

perhaps using simple mechanisms to make the pop-up parts move. Your library or local bookshop may stock pop-up books; some are very imaginative and you can look through them for ideas.

Resource Links

The Drawing and Modelling section has advice on equipment and materials to use for pop-ups.

The Mechanisms section in Resources for Understanding, and the mechanical toy project on page 18, may help you with ideas.

Spinning games

Ron, Annabel, Weng and Agnes all belong to the board-games club held after school. They are particularly keen on fantasy role-play games. As other people use the games they often find that some of the dice are missing. This is made worse by the fact that one of their favourite games needs three dice. They decide to design and make a spinner that can count up to 20 which they can use instead of dice. Their design will need to be cheat-proof and it should produce numbers randomly for each 'throw'. They want it to be too large to be lost easily but small enough to store. The style and appearance must be in tune with the fantasy games they play.

Figure 3 *Can you beat the dungeon master?*

The board-games club has been invited to put on a 'games evening' for the local old age pensioners. The leader has explained that the members like to play communal games. As their small spinner was successful Jon and his friends have been asked to design a large spinner for team quiz games.

It's the same every week — we spend half an hour looking for the dice!

ACTIVITIES

1 Are simple spinners as good as dice? Design and make some spinners and compare their performance with six-sided dice.

2 One way to avoid the problem that losing dice presents is to replace the dice with spinners that are designed into the game box. Try this for a game of your choice.

3 A spinner fitted into a box could also incorporate simple sound or light effects. Explore ways to do this.

4 Some people have made a fortune by designing and marketing a new board game, like 'Trivial Pursuit' for instance. Try designing a new game yourself. Remember that you will have to work out a set of rules, the layout of the board, designs for the counters and spinners or dice and the packaging, as well as the basic idea of the game. You might find it useful to work with a group of friends for a project like this. You will also need

We should design some dice that can't get lost!

to work out how to share the profits if the game is a commercial success!

5 Develop a design for a large-scale spinner that can be used with the old age pensioners. It will need to be portable, clearly visible and easy to dismantle.

6 Spinning tops are simply large-scale spinners but they can provide hours of fun for children of all ages. The bigger they are, the more difficult they are to spin. Try designing simple spinning tops and devise different ways to get them spinning.

Resource Links

If you decide to design and make spinners or spinning games it will be worth looking at the following sections. Electricity and Electronics, and Microelectronics will give you ideas on light and sound effects;
Energy, and Mechanisms, will help you think about ways to spin the spinner other than by using your fingers;
Showing Others in Drawing and Modelling will give you ideas on presentation graphics that will be useful for board and packaging.

Music makers

ACTIVITIES

Musical sounds can be made in the following ways:

- banging blocks (as in a xylophone);
- plucking stretched strings (as in a guitar);
- blowing air into or across pipes (as in a recorder or flute).

For one of these sound-makers, investigate the features which affect the type of sound. Is it the shape or size of the material 'banged'? Do different materials make different noises? Does the tension of a string affect the note? What about the thickness of the string? Does the diameter of a pipe affect the noise it makes? You will need to work with other people as there is lots to find out. You will also need to plan your investigations carefully so that you do not duplicate others' work.

You may find that the sound produced is not as loud as you would like. One of the simplest ways to amplify sound is to attach a hollow sound box to the instrument. You will need to investigate how the size, shape and material of the sound box affect its performance.

Once you understand one of the ways to make a musical sound you can begin to design your own musical instrument. It is important that your design takes into account both the way the instrument works and what you want it to look like. Both of these will be affected by the materials you choose and the overall form of your design. If you want a hi-tech appearance you will use different materials from those chosen for a classical or traditional appearance.

Resource Links

The following sections may be useful: Shapes and Sizes with details of hand size; Electricity and Electronics which shows ways to make musical notes and includes the circuit diagram for a simple electronic organ; Materials which will give you an overview of the forms of materials that might be available.

Once you have made your instruments you can compose a short piece and surprise your music teacher!

Puppet theatre

Julie, Ron, Darren and Annabel were asked by their youth club leader to put on a show for sick children at the local hospital. They were keen to do it and decided on a puppet show. Their first decision was about the story. Should they write it themselves or should they use one already written? Should it be traditional, like Punch and Judy, or modern? Their second decision was about the sort of puppets to use. They had a wide choice – finger or glove puppets, stick puppets, string puppets and shadow puppets were all possible. Their third decision was about the puppet theatre. It would have to be easy to carry and quick to set up. It would need curtains and scenery. Lighting and sound effects might also be needed. They decided to publicise the show in advance so that the children could look forward to it.

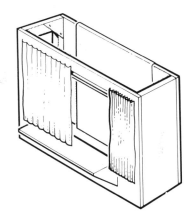

Figure 2 *You will need to make sure that your puppets fit the stage*

Figure 1 *There are many forms of puppet*

ACTIVITIES

Producing the puppets, theatre and story for a short play requires a lot of hard work. It is best tackled by a team. Write your own story for a performance that lasts 5 minutes. State the audience you are writing for and explain why you think your story will appeal to them.

Decide which sorts of puppet you will need and use the illustrations in Fig. 1 to design the characters in your story. You will find suggestions for puppet special effects on page 97.

Use the information on building frameworks on page 117 to help you design and make a strong but light theatre. Use the Mechanisms section on page 93 to help you design ways to move the curtains and change scenery.

More about survival

There are many everyday situations where danger is not far away. For example, it's fun to run along the sea front when the tide is in and great waves are splashing against the sea wall. Most of us have enjoyed dodging the spray and laughing at friends who don't quite manage it. However it's no laughing matter when someone slips through the railings. They have to be rescued before they are dragged under or swept out to sea. Designing a safe sea front, with easy-to-use rescue equipment, presents designers with an interesting challenge.

ACTIVITIES

1 Fig. 1 shows a safety railing along the sea wall after a very rough high tide. This railing has the important job of preventing people from falling into the sea, without obscuring the view. It must be made from materials held together in a

Figure 2 *How can you get the lifebelt to the person in danger?*

structure that is strong and stiff enough to resist the battering of the sea and its corrosive properties. The railings must be easy to mend.

Develop designs for a safety rail that looks better than the railings in the picture and which is just as safe (and if possible, more safe). Present clear sketches plus notes, and a scale model.

Points to think about:

a which materials would you choose if your design was made for real? Explain why.
b What form of material – solid, tube, angle section – would be best? Explain why.
c Explain how you decided on the height of the railings and size of any 'gaps'.
d How would your design be held together if it was made for real? Is it easy to repair?

2 Fig. 3 shows a lifebelt that can be thrown to people who are in difficulties in the sea. A simple device to throw a lifebelt out to sea could be very useful in an emergency. It should be easy to aim, simple to fire and it should be accurate over a range of distances up to 100 m. The lifebelt should carry with it a rope so that once the person in danger has got hold of the lifebelt he or she can be pulled to shore without too much risk to the rescuer.

Develop designs for a lifebelt-thrower using elastic bands as the energy source for the throwing. Present your first ideas as quick sketches, and from these build a small scale simple model that can throw a 50 mm diameter plasticine lifebelt a distance of 5 m. Test and modify your model to improve its accuracy and length of throw.

Figure 1 *Rough sea is very powerful*

Figure 3 *Dodging the spray can be fun*

When the sun shines lots of people of all ages enjoy being outside doing outdoor activities. The most popular is probably just sitting or lying in the sun. As it is hot most people wear shorts and T-shirts or swimming costumes. Dressed like this it is very easy to be exposed to too much sun without realising. The results can range from mild sunburn (only slightly painful) to severe sunburn (very painful) and sunstroke. These sometimes need treatment from a doctor and really bad cases may require admission to hospital.

ACTIVITIES

It is particularly important to protect your eyes from the glare of bright sunlight. Can you design a one piece, easy-to-assemble, cardboard hat that will give the required protection and which can be worn by both adults and children?

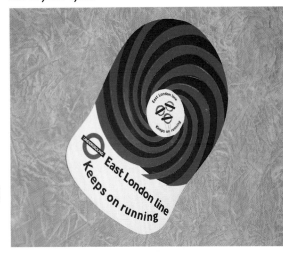

Figure 4 *Will something like this keep the sun out of your eyes?*

Figure 5 *Most people enjoy the sunshine*

Points to think about:

a how much does the size of heads vary? What are the smallest and largest sizes that can be used for the hat?
b Can you make the hat adjustable so that it fits on all people in this size range?
c What shape is best to give shade to the eyes?
d What shape is best to hold the hat on the head?
e How can these shapes be combined and then drawn on to a flat sheet that can be cut out and assembled into the 3D shape needed for the hat?
f How can the shape be designed to use the least possible amount of card? If possible, limit your design to a single sheet of A4 card.
g How can you make your design attractive to wear? Should it be brightly coloured? Should it advertise a popular product so that it is trendy? Would some colours be better at reflecting sunlight than others?
h It is always worth looking at how other people have tackled a design challenge. Fast-food stores often give away card hats as part of their advertising and you will learn a lot about making 3D shapes from flat card by looking at them carefully.

What you need to produce:

a a series of paper mock-ups showing how your early ideas developed into your final design;
b a series of coloured sketches showing different ways to make your design attractive;
c a single card showing the hat as it might be bought from a shop, and an assembled hat;
d a short report describing how you tested the hat and whether it meets the challenge.

More about wind energy

Wind energy is very important in the developing world because it is cheap. It can be used to drive a windmill to operate pumps that supply water to crops. It is important that both the windmill and the pump are simple, reliable and easy to maintain. It is also important that the windmill works with light winds coming from any direction. A very windy region would be unsuitable for growing most crops. Fig. 2 shows a wind pump that is used in Kenya. The pump is produced by the Intermediate Technology Group.

The simplest sort of pump is shown in Fig. 1. It is called a *positive displacement pump*. The valves open and close as shown to lift water up to the surface. Clearly a mechanism of some kind is needed to connect the rotating shaft of the windmill to the pump. One possibility is to use a crank and connecting rod like those shown in Fig. 3. As the crank rotates, the connecting rod will move the pump up and down. You may have other ideas. Designing a wind pump that helps people grow food in dry places is an important design challenge.

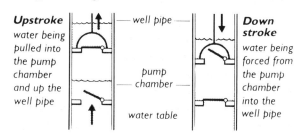

Upstroke water being pulled into the pump chamber and up the well pipe	well pipe — pump chamber water table	**Down stroke** water being forced from the pump chamber into the well pipe

Figure 1 *A simple displacement pump*

Figure 2 *Wind pump in Africa*

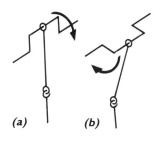

(a)   (b)

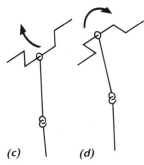

(c)   (d)

Figure 3 *Round-and-round to up-and-down*

ACTIVITIES

Consider whether Julie's windmill on page 30 could be developed into a small-scale prototype for a windpump.

Points to think about:

a *How to model the pump.*
You can use clear acrylic tube for the well pipe. This will enable you to see what's going on inside. You can cut discs from acrylic sheet for the valves and valve holders.
You could make the hinges for the valves from a flexible material that can be glued to the acrylic. You can use a bowl of water for the underground water.

b *How to use wind from any direction.*
One way to do this is to use a fan tail as shown.

> ## *Resource Links*

c *How to connect the pump to the windmill.*
Use Mechanisms (page 92–95) and Mechanical Systems (page 120) for help.

As this design challenge is quite complex it will be worth working in a team.

What you need to produce:

a a series of sketches and notes showing how you developed, tested and modified your pump to get the best performance;
b a series of sketches and notes showing how you modified Julie's design;
c a working model wind pump;
d a test report on the model wind pump.

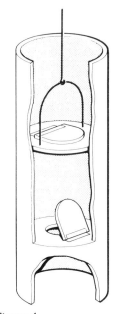

Figure 4
One way to model the pump

Figure 5
How to use the wind whatever its direction

How do people predict the weather? Well, it is important to know about the wind speed and direction, amongst other things. Weather stations have instruments to measure these. Many schools have their own small weather station which is used most often by the Geography department. You could design simple devices for a school weather station. They must be easy to use, reliable and made from cheap materials.

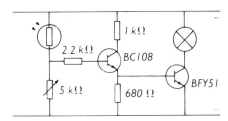

Figure 7 *Can you use this circuit to measure wind speed?*

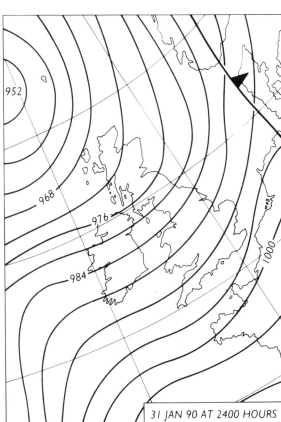

Figure 6 *Weather forecasting requires wind data*

31 JAN 90 AT 2400 HOURS

Figure 8 *You can build a cup anemometer like this*

ACTIVITIES

The anemometer shown in Fig. 8 spins round in the wind. The faster the wind, the faster it spins round. It catches wind from any direction. The problem is that the anemometer usually spins round so fast that it is not possible to distinguish between different wind speeds. The detector circuit shown in Fig. 7 will make the signal lamp flash every time a light is shone onto the light dependent resistor (LDR). It should be possible to attach a disc with a hole in it to the shaft of the anemometer. The signal lamp will flash every time the shaft rotates. This should give a flashing rate that depends on the wind speed. If the light is flashing so fast that it appears to be on all the time, then it may be necessary to use gears to slow down the speed of the rotating detector disc.

Points to think about:

a which material will you use to form the anemometer cups?
b How will you attach the cups to the central shaft?
c How will you support the central shaft?
d How will you attach the detector disc to the rotating shaft?
e Will you use a single container for the detecting disc and circuit? Or are there any advantages in having two containers, one for the anemometer and detector and another for the detecting circuit?
f Where will you position the flashing signal lamp?

What you need to produce:

a notes and sketches showing how you developed your anemometer design;
b notes and sketches showing how you built and tested the detector circuit;
c a working anemometer;
d notes and sketches describing how you tested and modified the anemometer to get the clearest indication of wind speed from the flashing lamp.

Figure I Shops designed for a busy station

More about shops

Recently the forecourts in large railways stations have been developed as shopping precincts to provide services for travellers. Shops were first placed around the edges of the entrance hall. To begin with these consisted of newsagents and fast food outlets. Soon afterwards clothes shops, chemists, off-licences and photolabs came on the scene. It was not long before all the available 'round the edge' sites had been used up. In most large entrance halls there are pillars supporting the roof of the hall. At several stations these have been used to provide a central support for shops; a bit like a tent pole only the tent is made of an aluminium framework and glass panels. This innovative idea provides more space for shops and, unlike many of the 'around-the-edge' shops, there is room to walk around inside. It is difficult to imagine how you could fit any more permanent shop space into station foyers.

ACTIVITIES

I Visit your local main line station and make brief sketches of the different shops that are there. (You could also take photos.) Present the sketches as a display with notes to show the following:

- the range of facilities,
- the different styles of shop and how this depends on what they sell,
- the uniforms worn by sales staff,
- the logos of different 'chain' shops.

2 Imagine that you have the job of designing one of the following shops which will have a place on every main line station entrance hall in the country:

florist, newsagent, sock or tie shop, shoe repairer, photolab, chemists.

You will need to draw several shopfront views and sketch different ways of making them attractive to customers. If there is time you might be able to develop a stand-up 3D model complete with sales staff in uniforms that you have designed.

Do you ever shop at a supermarket? Going there for a week's shopping is very different to buying a few groceries from a corner store. Pushing a heavy, loaded trolley along the aisles and queueing for what seems hours in order to pay is not what most people enjoy. But lots of people do use supermarkets because despite their drawbacks they are very convenient. Supermarkets sell a very wide range of goods on a self-service basis. Most of the staff that the customers come into contact with are employed to operate the check-out tills and to restock the shelves. Only very few of the staff, if any, have to deal with customer enquiries. There appears to be very little 'active' selling. It is the layout of the goods and the ways in which they are packaged and displayed that will, to a large extent, govern how successful the supermarket is. Very little of this is left to chance.

3 Working as a group, visit a local grocery supermarket and gather the following information:

■ a layout plan with the type of goods sold on each stand clearly marked;

■ the positions of the main signs telling customers where particular types of goods can be found;
■ a front view of one or two stands noting where goods are placed – high, low and mid-way;
■ details of the supermarket's logo or brand image with notes on where it is used;
■ a list of the different numbers of brands of the same product that are on sale, eg. baked beans or cornflakes and the prices charged.

Present this information as a group display and, working on your own, use it to answer the following questions.

a Make a list of groceries for your family's weekly shopping. Using this list and a copy of the layout plot the route required to buy all the goods. Present this route as clearly as possible. How much of the supermarket do you see as you travel round buying the things that you need?
b List the main signs used to classify areas of the store. Was anything on your list difficult to find using these signs? Could you see all the signs from anywhere in the store?
c Can you explain why certain goods are placed high, others low and some mid-way?
d How instantly recognizable is the supermarket logo or brand image?
e What governs the prices charged for different brands of the same product? Find out what *brand loyalty* means.

Figure 2 *Inside a large supermarket; you almost need a map!*

Convenience food

ACTIVITIES

Make a list of all the different take-away foods that you can buy in your area. Collect samples of the packaging used for each. For each one try to answer the following questions.

a Does the packaging survive a journey in a shopping basket, on a car seat, in a saddle bag?
b Does the packaging break when dropped from hand height?
c If the contents leak, does the packaging become weak or disintegrate?
d If the packaging gets wet does it become weak or disintegrate?
e Does the packaging look good?
f Is it instantly clear that the product has come from a particular shop?
g Does it keep hot food and drink warm?
h Does it keep cold food and drink cool?
i Are the materials biodegradable?
j Are the materials environment-friendly?

Convenience food has become popular in recent years. Sometimes people are too busy or simply do not want to spend time preparing and cooking meals. Containing and packaging convenience food offers many challenges for the designer.

'Take-aways' offer a wide variety of 'fast food' and you can now order food (like pizzas) over the telephone and have it delivered to your home. The food must be kept hot and moist while it is being transported so the container should be made from a material that is a good insulator. The material used should be able to stand up to the temperature of the food without softening or melting. It should also resist rain.

Food containers that go in the oven must withstand very high temperatures. Until recently,

Figure 1 *Take-away packaging*

Figure 2 *A TV dinner*

ready-prepared meals were sold in aluminium foil containers but now they also come in containers that are made from a heat-resistant plastic that will not soften when it is heated.

Some containers have to be designed to hold a whole meal so the container must have compartments for different foods or courses. Aeroplane meals are a good example. The container must be strong enough to resist damage during transportation and stacking. It must also be large enough to contain the food without spilling during turbulent conditions. Yet it must be compact because the meal has to be eaten in a confined space. The space available on the plane for storing the containers is also very limited. These containers are usually made from sheet plastic that can be heated and vacuum-formed.

ACTIVITIES

Design and make a fast food container from card. When assembled from flat it should act like a tray to hold a meal of a hamburger, chips and a drink in separate compartments. The shapes and sizes of the compartments will need careful planning to make the best use of the space. You will need to measure the hamburger and other contents if you are to do this properly.

Resource Links ▷

Use the Drawing and Modelling section on page 63 to help you.

To find out about conducting and insulating materials, turn to the Energy and Materials sections of Resources for Understanding.

The Forming section, page 113 in Resources for Action, will give useful information about using vacuum-forming on plastics.

Carrying sports gear

draw a clear sketch and mark in important sizes.
b Make a scale drawing of a bicycle and mark in those places where sports gear might be carried.
c Compare the spaces available (from **2**) with the spaces needed (from **1**). Now that you have some idea of where different items might be carried you can think about ways of holding these onto the bicycle. You will need to ask yourself the following questions.

- How firmly do I need to hold the equipment?
- Can I buy ready-made clips?
- How easy should these clips be to do up and undo?
- How can I ensure they don't interfere with riding or steering the bicycle?
- How can I ensure they don't weaken the frame of the bicycle?

d Use sketches and notes to answer these questions and develop possible designs. You might find it useful to model your ideas in card.
e You should only try to make your best design when you have produced a model, checked it thoroughly and modified it if necessary.

Resource Links

The following Resource sections might be useful to answer the questions above:

Shapes and Sizes, page 78;
Joining materials, page 114;
Drawing and Modelling (Thinking It Through), page 66.

ACTIVITIES

You can tackle Julie's problem in the following stages.

a Make a list of the different sorts of sports gear you might want to carry on a bike. For each item

Warnings

Darren and Agnes decided to take Rose, Agnes' niece, on a visit to the zoo. It was the first time they had taken a small child on the Underground and they were a bit worried about how they would cope. Their first problem was getting down the escalator – the pushchair had to be carried. On the platform they nearly got on the wrong train; Agnes noticed the 'correction' display just in time. As they got on the train the public address system told them to 'Mind the gap' and 'Stand clear of the doors'. At the zoo they had to keep a sharp eye on Rose to make sure she didn't feed the animals or put her hands through the bars. Darren and Agnes' trip was full of warning signs. Some were posters, others were electronic displays, while others were announcements. Warnings are different from alarm signals. A warning is designed to prevent an accident or mishap. An alarm signal is designed to let people know that something has *already* happened.

ACTIVITIES

Your surroundings will be full of warning signs. The list on the right shows some places you could look to find them. Make careful sketches with notes to record what they look like and exactly where they are placed and use these to decide if the warning signs are effective:

Help!

- on the road for both drivers and pedestrians;
- in places where there are large numbers of people – eg. cinemas, theatres, pop concerts and rallies;
- in places where people go to do dangerous things – eg. swimming pools and sports centres;
- in places where there are hazardous materials – eg. filling stations;
- on the packaging of products that might cause injury;
- in places of work where machinery is operating.

Resource Links

If you decide to produce some warning signs it will be worth looking at the following:

Drawing and Modelling Showing Others – this will help you make sure that the warning sign is clear and stands out;
Shapes and Sizes – this will help you to position the warning so that all concerned can see it;
Materials – it will be important to use materials that are long-lasting and easily cleaned;
Electricity and Electronics, and Microelectronics – these will give you more ideas on how to make the warning stand out;
Puppet theatre, Problems with play and Moisture sensor projects described in this book can all include warning design.

SHOWING WHAT'S INSIDE YOUR HEAD

When you tackle a design problem, it is important to put all your ideas down on paper at an early stage. It is easier to sort out your ideas from a series of sketches than to try and compare them all in your head. Drawing is also the best way of recording your thoughts and ideas before they are forgotten!

Getting ideas for your projects in the first place can be a problem, and the first two sections of this book will suggest where and how you can start. This section will show you how to improve your drawing and modelling skills.

What to use

■ PAPER

Paper for design sketching should be white or off-white, and have a smooth but not shiny surface. Most paper sizes are part of the 'A' series. Each size fits exactly twice into the next size up. This book is A4 size. It is best to work on either A4, which is a good size for carrying in a bag, or on A3, which will allow you to make many more drawings and written notes on one sheet. A small sketchbook is handy for jotting down ideas when you are not in a design room.

■ ERASERS

Smudges and mistakes on pencil work can be rubbed out with either a plastic or soft 'putty' eraser. You can avoid a lot of smudging by making sure that your hands are clean before you start and by keeping your drawing hand away from completed pencil work.

■ PENCILS

Pencils are graded according to their hardness or softness. A soft pencil will give a darker line than a hard pencil. Hardness is graded 'H', softness is graded 'B'. Softer pencils such as 2B or 4B do not need as much pressure to make a line, so are good for freehand drawing and shading. Pencils used for outlining and writing notes should always have a fine point. For outlining, use a B or 2B. For writing notes, use an H or HB. Use a good pencil sharpener, a blunt one will break your lead.

■ FINE-LINE MARKERS

Fine-line markers can be used like a pencil for quick sketches and notes, yet also give a thin bold line like a technical pen. The lines do not rub out so, until you feel more confident, it is probably best to practise your drawing skills using a soft pencil.

Freehand drawing

Freehand drawing is the quickest way of getting your ideas onto paper. This means drawing without the aid of equipment such as rulers, set-squares or compasses. If you do not feel confident about your drawing ability, don't be put off. There are simple techniques that you can practise to help improve your skills.

STARTING OFF

- Practise drawing some clean straight lines using two dots to aim between. Move your whole arm rather than twisting your wrist.
- Try to vary the pressure on the pencil to get lighter and darker, or thicker and thinner lines.
- Draw some sets of parallel lines, both straight and curved. For the curved lines you will find it helps to move your wrist.

SKETCHING

- When you start to sketch, keep your pencil lines faint. This way you can alter the length or direction of a line slightly without having to keep rubbing out. When you are satisfied with a shape, go over it with a bolder line.
- If your object is a difficult shape to draw, build it up from several simple shapes. Circles and rectangles drawn faintly are useful guides.
- When drawing symmetrical shapes, start by drawing a faint centre line. Make sure each line you draw is identical to the one opposite.

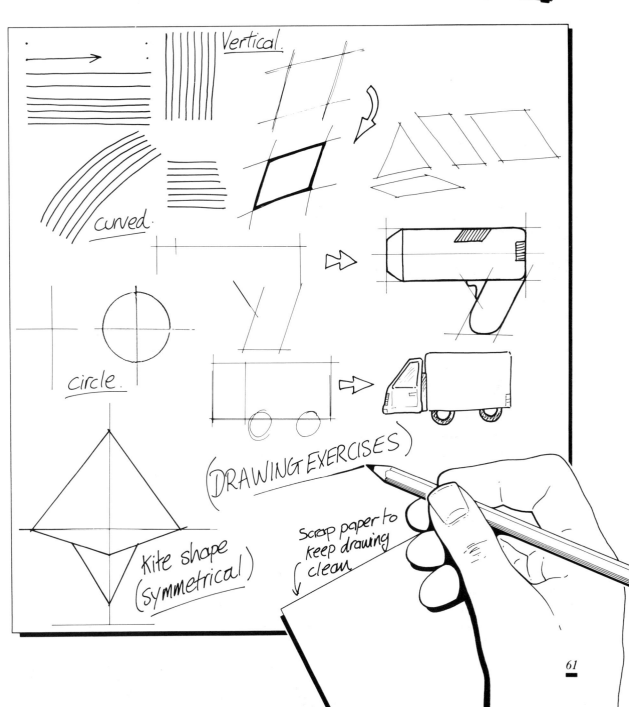

Shape

Many of your first design ideas can often be drawn using simple *shapes*. Shapes are formed when a space is enclosed by a *line*. The lines around the shapes are the *outlines*. You can see from these examples that most of the ideas have been drawn as flat, two-dimensional shapes. A 2D shape has only two dimensions or measurements – *length* and *width*.

Most of Lisa's ideas for her piece of personal adornment were drawn as *top* or *plan* views. It would be made of thin sheet material so she wanted to concentrate on interesting shapes that could be cut from it.

Annabel drew up a flow chart to help her decide what shape the body of her toy person transporter should be. Another method would be to draw the different vehicle shapes. Why would a *side* view be the most suitable in this case? Why is it important that all the vehicles should be drawn from the same angle?

Darren had several ideas for his shop design besides the one that he decided to develop. He concentrated on drawing *front* views because he wanted to show how the names and logos would appear on his design.

Form

Most of the designs on page 62 are 'flat', or two-dimensional shapes. They have two dimensions, length and width. Most people find it quite easy to draw 2D shapes and, as you have seen, this kind of drawing is sometimes enough to record and show your ideas. However, when we look at real objects, we see their form in three dimensions – length, width, and thickness. By cutting and folding a flat shape on paper or card we can create a 3D form.

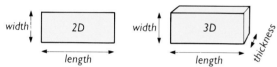

Figure 1 *How shape is different to form*

Fig. 2 shows an arrangement of shapes which together could be cut out of card and folded to make a 3D form of Annabel's transporter. This flat version of the design is called a *development*. *Tabs* have been added to the main shapes to help join the pieces together.

Another way of modelling ideas is to use *Plasticine*. When experimenting with different forms for a piece of personal adornment, Lisa found Plasticine to be a quick way of visualising the ideas. The Plasticine could be remodelled very easily, and reused many times.

Sometimes a flat, 2D view does not show enough information about the object you are drawing. A 3D view or pictorial sketch is needed instead.

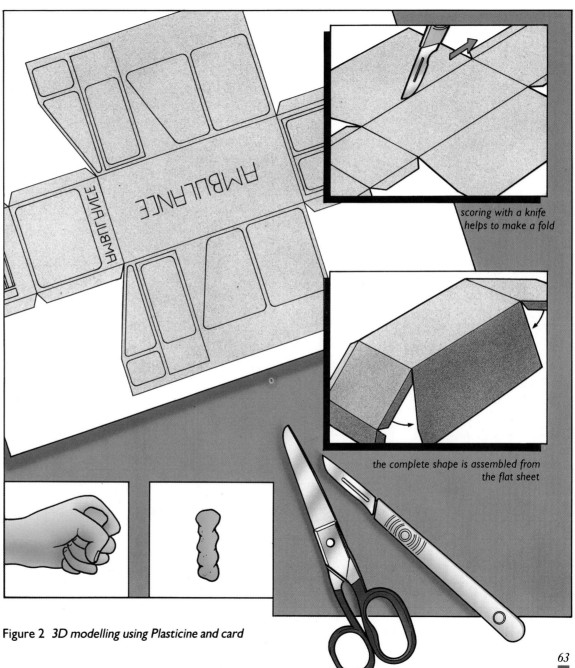

scoring with a knife helps to make a fold

the complete shape is assembled from the flat sheet

Figure 2 *3D modelling using Plasticine and card*

Showing 3D

The quickest and easiest way of producing a 3D view is to start with a flat, front view of the object, as shown in Figure 1. Then draw parallel lines from the corners of the shape, at 45° to the horizontal, keeping them about the same length. Joining up these lines will give you a 3D form. If you have some squared paper, you can draw your shape using the grid as a guide. The squares will also help you aim your diagonal lines at a 45° angle. If the grid lines are not faint, you could draw on thin paper clipped over the squared paper, as shown in Fig. 1. Keep all your sketched lines faint until you are sure that you have drawn the correct lines – then go over the outlines.

This type of drawing is called an *oblique view*. Because oblique views are based on flat front views, they are an easy way of drawing circular or curved forms.

GRIDS

Other types of grid paper can be used to help you sketch freehand, and some examples are shown in Fig. 2. Some grids are printed in light blue or green and do not show up when photocopied, leaving only your drawing on the paper.

Figure 1 *Turning flat shapes into 3D*

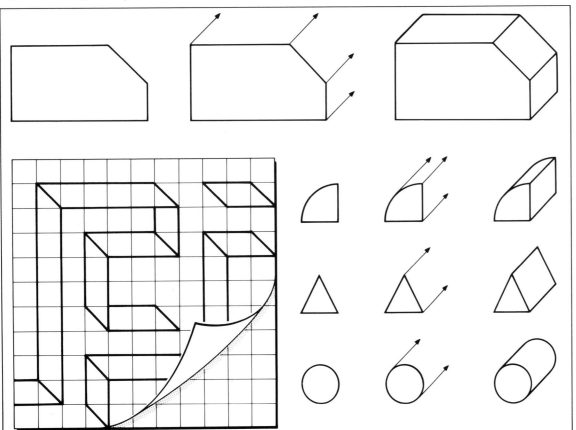

Figure 2 *Grids to help you show 3D form*

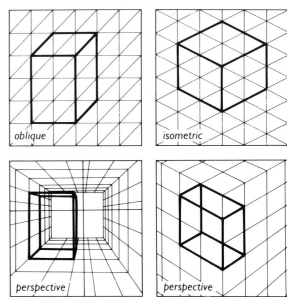

oblique

isometric

perspective

perspective

Crating

Drawing a box or 'crate' in 3D can be the basis for drawing many other objects. This method of drawing is called *crating*.

The best way to begin is to imagine that the object you wish to draw is packed inside one or more boxes. When you have decided on a suitable view, the framework of the box can be lightly drawn in. It may be helpful to add other construction lines, like centre lines or lines dividing the boxes up into sections. Finally, you can sketch in the object itself, adding details and outlining when you are satisfied with the drawing.

Annabel drew a number of crates like these when she was sketching ideas for her toy people transporter. She knew that the overall shape was going to be close to a rectangular box.

Figure 3 *Crating will help you develop ideas in 3D*

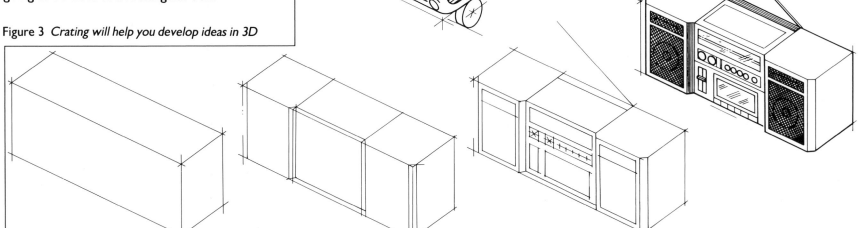

THINKING IT THROUGH

Enlarging and reducing

Sometimes you may want to enlarge or reduce the size of a shape for a design drawing. A simple method involves using a *grid* (Fig. 1). A grid can either be drawn directly over the original shape, or drawn onto tracing paper and then placed over the shape you wish to copy.

To *enlarge*, draw another grid, larger than the original, but divided into the same number of squares. To *reduce*, draw the second grid smaller, but also divided into the same number of squares.

The original shape can now be drawn freehand onto the second grid, plotting carefully the points where each line crosses the grid. If the picture is very detailed, the grid can be divided into smaller squares to give more plotting points.

Figure 1 *You can use a grid to enlarge a diagram*

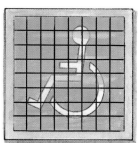

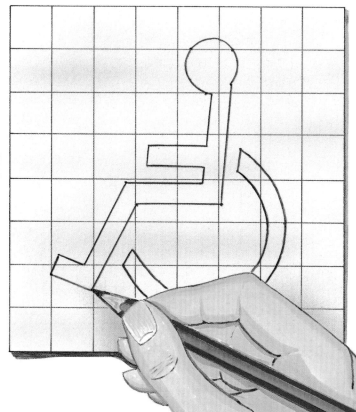

OTHER METHODS

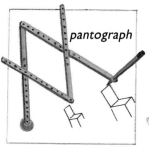
pantograph

photocopier

overhead projector

episcope

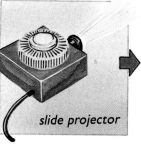
slide projector

Figure 2 *Other ways to enlarge your design*

There are a number of other ways to enlarge or reduce a picture or shape. Some of them involve projecting the image through a lens and then drawing round the enlarged version. A *pantograph* can enlarge or reduce, but takes some practice to use. Some photocopiers enlarge and/or reduce images which can then be traced.

Detail drawing

It is easy to overlook the smaller details of a design project especially if they are not clearly seen on sketches. These details need to be thought out just as carefully as other parts of a project. It is a good idea to draw some larger sketches of them to help you sort out your ideas.

Drawing a circular frame can suggest that the detail is being viewed through a magnifying glass. Weng drew some magnified sketches of the linkages on his kite frame to help work out how the different pieces were going to join together. He drew a few different versions so that he had a clearer idea about which was the best solution.

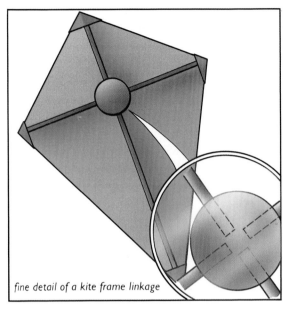

fine detail of a kite frame linkage

Figure 3 *Weng's detail drawing of his kite*

HIDDEN DETAIL

Details which cannot normally be seen may be shown on a drawing in a number of ways.

- Thin broken lines can be used to show the outline of a shape inside an object.
- Ghosting – imagine that the skin of the object is transparent. The detail inside can then be drawn in.
- Cut-aways – part of the surface of the object can be shown cut or peeled away to show the inside.

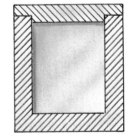

Figure 4 *Inside a cosmetics package*

SECTIONAL VIEWS

Sometimes details are not just small they are completely hidden. In this case it is useful to imagine your design has been cut through or sectioned. You can then draw what you would see.

The sectional view in Fig. 4 shows a cosmetics container as if it has been sliced down the middle. This drawing shows the detail inside the container. Fig. 4 also shows a flat view showing the true shape. This is called a *cross-section*.

- Notice that the exposed cut surfaces have been *hatched* with thin parallel lines at an angle of 45°. Where two different parts meet, the hatching is drawn in the opposite direction to avoid confusion.
- Sections can be made vertically (up and down), or horizontally (across) along an object.
- If the object is symmetrical, only half of it needs to be sectioned.

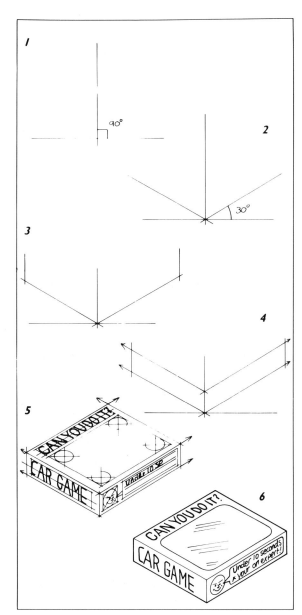

Figure 1 *How Ronabir used isometric drawings to design his package*

Isometric views

An *isometric view* is one way of showing three dimensions on a drawing. This kind of view can be drawn using special isometric grid paper or, with practice, you can sketch the objects freehand (see pages 64 and 65). It can be useful if you want to draw your idea more accurately and to scale so that you can work out some of the likely problems.

For an isometric view, the object is drawn at an angle with one corner being the closest point to the viewer. The height, width and length are shown as parallel sets of lines, and can be drawn to scale.

The step-by-step drawings show how Ronabir drew the maze game package as an isometric view to help him gain an idea of the right proportions to use.

In order to draw the view accurately and to scale, you will need to use some drawing instruments, some of which are shown in Fig. 2.

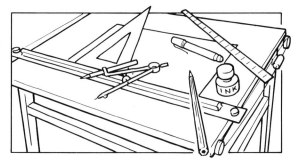

Figure 2 *You can use a drawing board and set square*

SKETCHING ELLIPSES

When a circular object is tilted, the shape that you see is no longer a circle but more of an oval shape or *ellipse*. It is quite difficult to draw ellipses freehand, so the guidelines below will help, especially if you practise.

Figure 3 *Drawing ellipses*

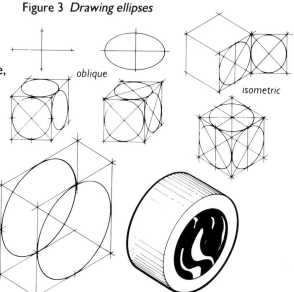

Exploded views

Drawing an *exploded view* can be a useful way of showing how your design will be put together. Although this title suggests an explosion, the drawing actually shows the object as if it were pulled apart. The different pieces are not scattered over the paper in a random way, but are laid out in an ordered fashion. This type of drawing is mostly made as a 3D view. You can see how Julie's windmill design is much easier to understand because of the exploded view, Fig. 5.

Figure 4 *Exploded view of a membrane panel switch*

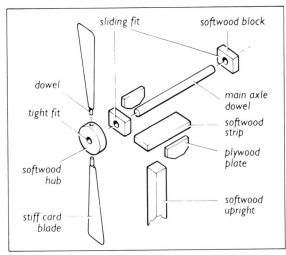

Figure 5 *Exploded view of Julie's windmill*

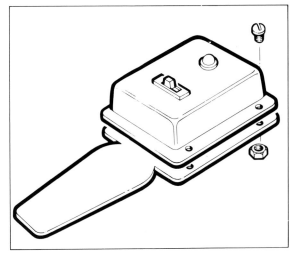

Figure 6 *Using thick and thin lines to give impact*

Thick and thin lines

If you compare the two drawings of Agnes' moisture sensor in Fig. 6 and on page 28, you will see that one has been improved by the addition of thicker lines. This technique of using different thicknesses of line is a simple way of giving your drawings more impact.

You can use the following rules to help you decide where to use thick and thin lines on your drawings:

- A thick line is added to an edge where only one surface is seen (Fig. 6).
- A line which shows two surfaces meeting on an edge is left thin.

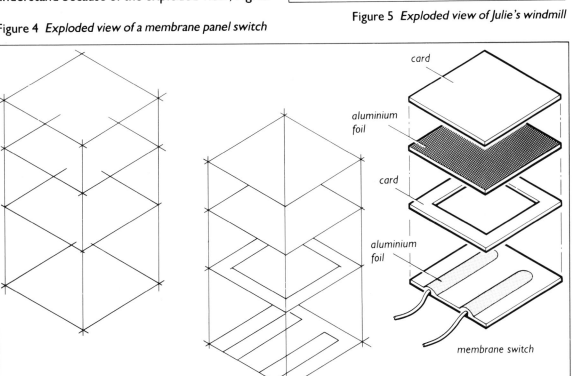

Model making

Making a model can be helpful in the early stages of solving a design problem. Quick and easily-made models can act as 3D sketches of design solutions. They can help you to see what your idea will look like, how it will work, and if there are any faults. It is better to discover a fault at this stage rather than later, when much time and effort may have been wasted.

On page 33, we saw how Darren used a card model to enable him to see his idea in 3D. Lisa used Plasticine to experiment with different forms for her personal adornment project. The models shown on this page have been made to help think the problem through.

Models that are smaller than life-size are useful when designing large items like furniture and room interiors. For example, they can be helpful when checking the stability of a structure, or the layout or colour scheme of a room.

Model-making is useful if your design involves moving parts, mechanisms, or circuits. For example, when Jon made his 2D moving toy, he needed to work out carefully how the movement would be made in order to get the best result.

Models that are larger than life-size can be useful when designing small items like jewellery or detailed mechanisms, especially to help explain how they will work.

A full-size model or mock-up can be essential for testing designs involving people, such as a seat or a hand-held device, for example.

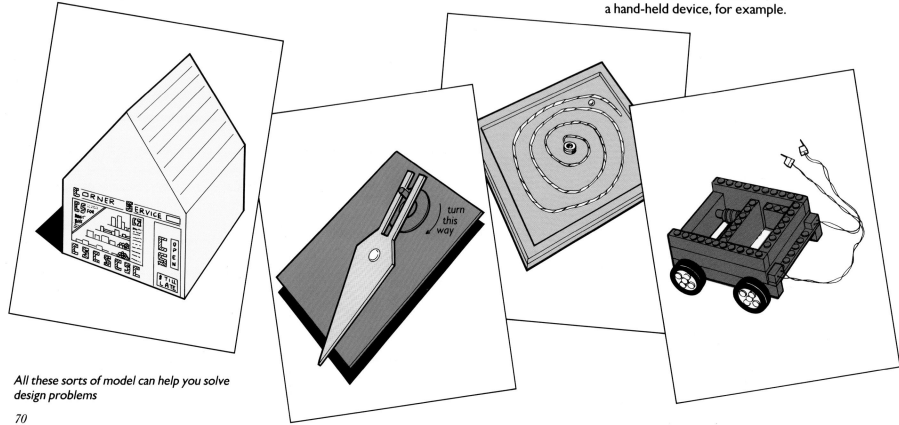

All these sorts of model can help you solve design problems

Model making materials

■ SHEET MATERIALS

- *Paper* – large range of colours, easy to cut and fold.
- *Card* – empty boxes, packaging, large range of colours and thicknesses.
- *Plastic* – polystyrene sheet, PVC, ABS.
- *Wood* – veneers, thin balsa, plywood and hardboard.

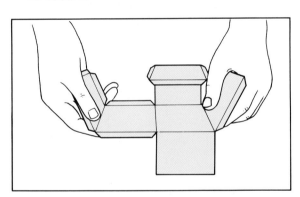

Figure 1 *You can turn sheet material into a box*

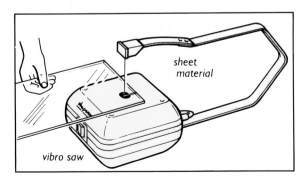

Figure 2 *You can cut sheet material with a vibrosaw*

■ FRAMEWORKS

- *Art straws* – larger than drinking straws.
- *String* – can be stiffened with glue.
- *Wire and welding rod* – thin wire can be bent easily; thicker wire and welding rod can be soldered to form frame.
- *Wood* – dowelling, balsa strips, off-cuts, cocktail sticks.
- *Construction kits* – Meccano, Fischer Technik, LEGO.

Figure 3 *You can make frameworks from special kits or ordinary materials*

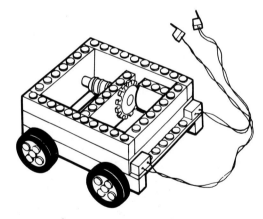

■ SOLID MATERIALS

- *Plasticine* – easy to form, can be reused.
- *Clay* – messy, but can be set hard.
- *Wood* – jelutong and balsa are light and easy to work with.
- *Plastic foams* – expanded polystyrene, styrofoam. Can be easily formed with hot wire cutter but beware of fumes.

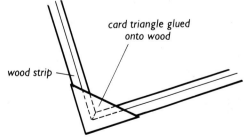

Figure 4 *Using a hot wire cutter*   Figure 5 *Covering a wire frame to make a shell*

■ FOUND MATERIALS

- *Packaging* – cans, bottles, polystyrene foam, card, cardboard tubes.
- *Wood off-cuts* – good for block models.
- *Plastic* – drainpipes, guttering.

Figure 6 *You can find lots of useful items*

SHOWING OTHERS

Working drawings

When you have decided on a solution to a design problem, you will need to make a *working drawing* showing all the measurements and details necessary for your design to be made. These drawings need to be clearly understood, not only by you but by anyone else who looks at them.

Figure 1 *This camera has six different sides*

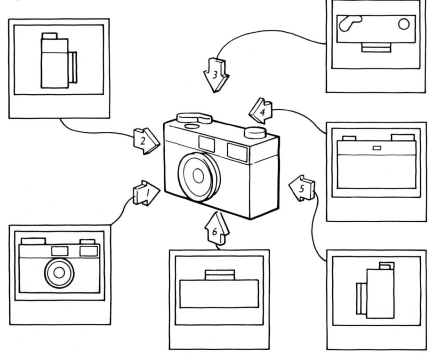

Working drawings usually show a series of flat, square-on views known as *orthographic views*. It is easier to draw your project from one direction at a time, and it can often be clearer, especially if you want to include measurements. Although there are six possible views to any object (Fig. 1), you need only usually draw three.

When drawing orthographic views, we refer to each as:

- *The plan* – the view looking down onto the object.
- *The front elevation* – the view that shows the most information.
- *The end elevation* – the remaining side view(s).

It is important to get the views in the right position, and in line with each other. It can help to imagine that the object is suspended inside a transparent box. If you imagine that you are looking through this box at the object, the views that you see can be traced onto the side of the box. If the box is opened out, the views will appear as shown in Fig. 2. Notice that the plan view is *above* the front view, and the left-hand view is placed to the left of the front view.

Using grid or graph paper will make it easier to line these views up with each other, (Fig. 2).

Figure 2 *You can draw an orthographic of the camera like this*

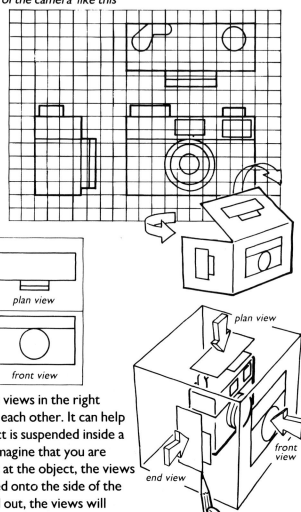

- If the object you are drawing is complex, you may need to show more than three views.
- Dimensions (sizes) and notes about materials and construction can be added to the drawing. Dimension lines should be thin, ending in an arrow, and just touching the limit lines. It is important that these lines are not confused with the outlines of the object.

- Hidden details can be shown using dotted lines (page 67).
- A 'Parts List' should be added to contain all the information about the materials, sizes and quantities needed.
- Adding a 3D view to this sheet may help to give an even clearer impression of the design.

Figure 3 *This personal stereo is complicated, a complete drawing will need more than three views. Adding dimensions makes the sizes clear. A parts list completes the description but a 3D view often gives a better impression.*

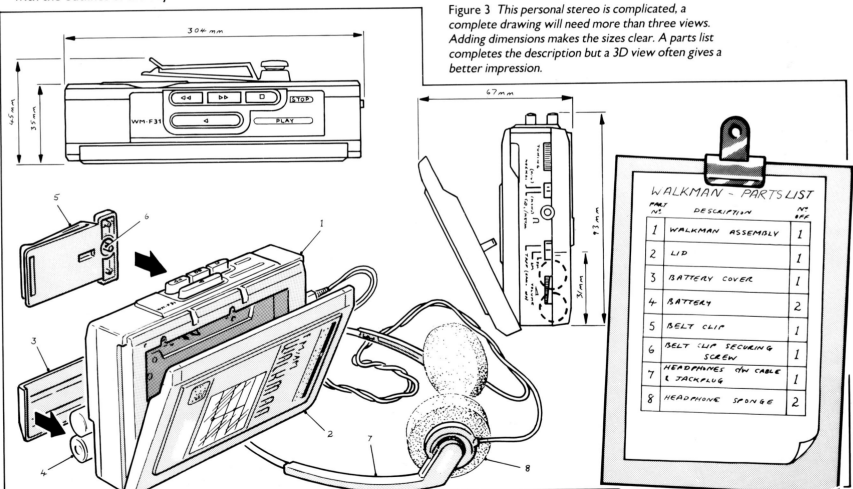

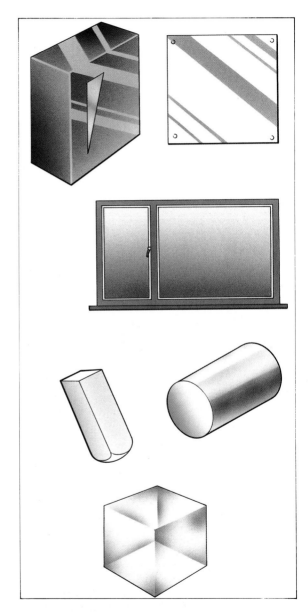

Materials and texture

Some of the surfaces of objects you draw will be shiny and smooth, while others will be dull and rough. It can be important to add these surface textures to your drawings to show others the kind of material you intend to use for a design.

The surface finish of different materials can be shown on a drawing using dots, lines, or contrasting areas of light and dark. Sometimes the material can be indicated by copying the surface texture (Fig. 1 and Fig. 2).

If you look carefully at the examples on this page, you will notice that the texturing has not been applied evenly all over the objects. Surfaces which are shaded from the light have been textured strongly, while those surfaces facing the light have little or no texture drawn on them. An even texture over the whole object will tend to make it look flat.

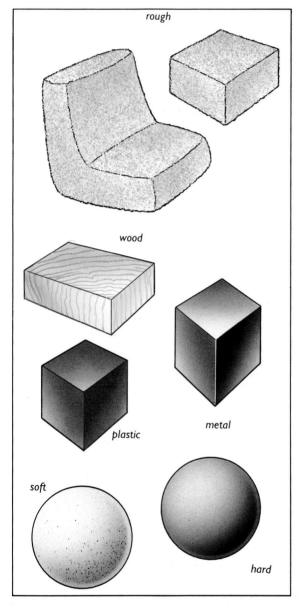

Figure 1 *You can show what surfaces are like by the way you draw them*

Figure 2 *You can use uneven shading to make your designs look real*

Perspective

Because perspective drawings are similar to how we actually see things in real life, they are often used to present ideas to others. If you look down a long straight road, you will see that the lamp posts and cars in the distance appear to be smaller. The road itself appears to get narrower until it disappears at a point – the vanishing point. A perspective drawing is a way of copying this illusion onto paper.

One-point perspective is the simplest type to draw because it is based on a 'flat' view of an object and ONE vanishing point. This is the imaginary point where the road appears to 'vanish'. This type of perspective drawing is often used to show room settings, stage sets, window displays or street scenes.

Figure 3 *We see things 'in perspective'*

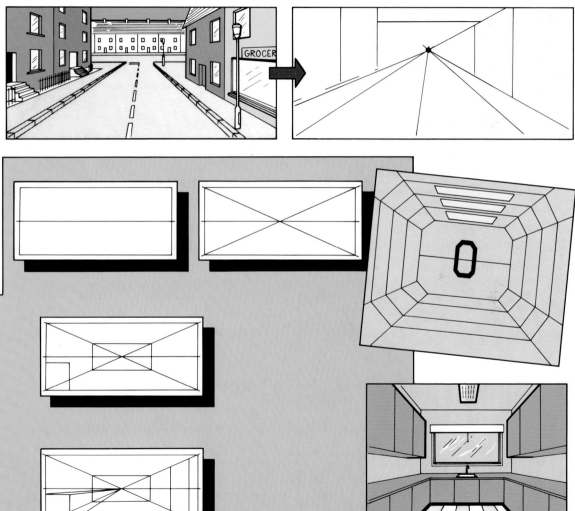

Figure 4 *You can draw one point perspective like this*

Lettering

Adding notes or headings to a drawing can be a good way of giving more information about a design idea. As well as making sure that other people understand your drawings, notes can also help to explain ideas that you are unable to draw.

■ HAND LETTERING

Hand lettering can be constructed between two *guidelines*. If your paper is thin enough, you could use lined or graph paper underneath as a guide. These guidelines can be varied in width to give different size letters. For larger letters, more than two guidelines can be used. Always use a soft pencil, at least HB, when drawing in the letter.

Figure 1 *Letters come in many styles*

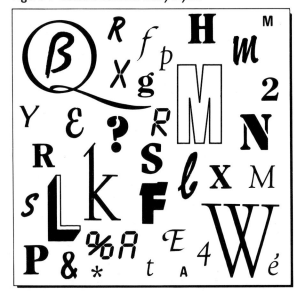

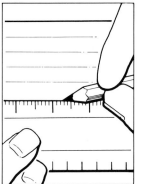

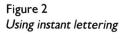

Figure 2
Using instant lettering

■ INSTANT LETTERING

'Dry Transfer' instant letters can give very neat, professional results for labels, headings and titles. As it can be expensive and time consuming to apply, this type of lettering is not really suitable for large blocks of words or notes. You may find it useful when designing the graphics for a package or boardgame, as there is a large range of letter styles to choose from.

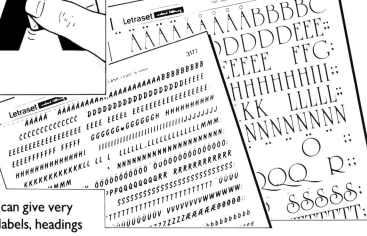

■ KEY POINTS

- Lettering should be added carefully to avoid spoiling the drawing.
- Avoid fancy letter styles. Keep letters simple so that the letters do not overpower the drawing.
- Different parts can be emphasised by changing the size, thickness, or colour of the letters.
- Notes usually look best when positioned in neat columns or blocks, rather than scattered at angles over the paper.
- You should be able to read notes without turning the drawing sheet around.

■ OTHER IDEAS FOR LETTERING

- *Stencils* – neat but time consuming. Good for labels.
- *Typewriters* – can be effective if cut out and neatly placed on the drawing.
- *Computer-generated lettering*

Presentation

One of the reasons for drawing and modelling a design idea is to enable you to show it to other people. So it is important that your ideas are well presented and easily understood. Below are some guidelines to help you.

- *Layout* is how letters and pictures are arranged on a page. Clean presentation and good layout will enhance your work.
- Your design sheets should tell the story of how you have arrived at a solution. This is easier to follow if all your sheets are *numbered, dated* and *titled*.

- When *mounting* a design drawing, try fixing it to a slightly bigger sheet of coloured paper to form a frame. Avoid very brightly coloured paper.

If you mount your work, it will look better

- If you are mounting work for display, keep the layout simple. One technique is to line up one or two edges of work with other pieces of work (or lettering). Some examples are given on this page, but there are many variations.

You can organise your design sheets to make an interesting display

- You can pick out certain drawings on a design sheet by emphasising the outline – either with a coloured pencil or with a neutral-coloured marker. Or you can draw a frame around the shape you wish to highlight.

Make sure you number, date and title your design sheets

You can highlight good ideas

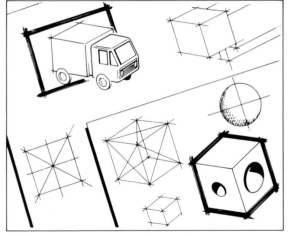

You can use a binder to keep the sheets in order

- Photographs are a good way of showing design situations, and can be added to or traced over to show a design solution.
- If your work involves textiles, colour schemes or even a slightly unusual material, adding some samples to your presentation will help to get the message across.

You can include material samples

You can use photographs to good effect

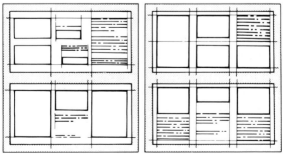

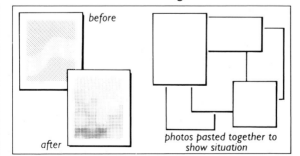

before

after

photos pasted together to show situation

RESOURCES

Shapes and sizes

VARIATION

People come in all shapes and sizes. If you look at the people in your class you will see that, even though you are all about the same age, there is a wide variation in what you are all like. There will be a range of heights, finger lengths, head sizes etc.. Everyone is different. This makes the job of designing things to be used by lots of different people quite tricky.

Scientists help designers by collecting information (data) about people's shapes and sizes. This data is called *anthropometrics*. There are large reference books filled with this information. The data given is always 'averaged' but it is important to remember that very few people are 'average'. To help solve this problem, the likely variation from the average for particular groups of people is usually given as well.

The data on body size alone is not enough to help the designer. It must be turned into useful information like – how high can people comfortably reach, or what height is suitable for a table? This sort of information is called *ergonomics*.

Figure 1 *Body size information useful to designers*

ACTIVITIES

If you were a jeweller you would need to measure the circumference of people's fingers. You can find out how much finger size varies in your class by using a piece of string to measure the circumference of everyone's third finger. You must be accurate, so the best unit to use is millimetres.

Present this information as a long list, with the largest measurement at the top and the smallest at the bottom. Then try to put sizes together into groups within 1 mm of each other. If you measure everyone's height as well you could see if there is any link between how tall people are and the size of their fingers. Is your data reliable enough to answer this question?

If you were making rings to sell to young people, what range of sizes would you choose?

Figure 2 *Note the similarities despite the differences*

Two very different bicycle designs are shown in Fig. 2. One is for general cycling and the other is for stunt riding. They must both be usable by a wide range of riders. The rider must be able to sit on the saddle with feet touching the ground. The rider must also be able to reach the handle bars and operate the brakes easily. The rider must be able to reach the pedals comfortably. Lots of differently-sized people will want to use one or other of these bicycles. It is only by the careful use of ergonomic and anthropometric data that designers have been able to produce two widely different machines that can be used by almost anybody.

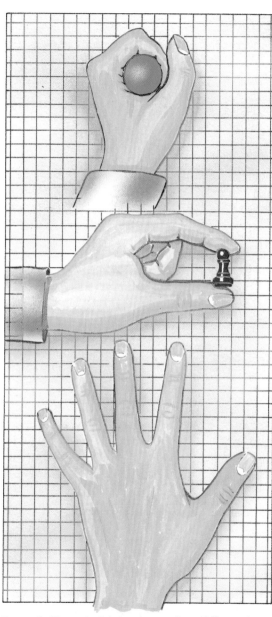

Figure 3 *Typical adult hand size – how different is yours? (One square represents 1 cm²)*

The human hand is a quite remarkable machine. It is capable of holding tools and using them with delicacy and precision, or with great power. Clearly designers have to understand exactly how the hand works, and its variation in size over the population, if they are to design handles correctly. Most of the things we use have handles (e.g. vacuum cleaners, saucepans, cups and mugs, cutlery, screwdrivers, cupboards and drawers, doors and windows) or are designed to be held (e.g. musical instruments, pocket radios, torches, showers, telephones). Recently, products with keyboards have become important (e.g. computers, calculators and personal organisers). If these are to be easy to use then the designer must understand how hands work.

ACTIVITIES

Make a list of the 'shape and size' data that you need for the following design situations:

- The untidy desk (page 36);
- Looks good to eat (page 37);
- Problems with play (page 40);
- Spinning games (page 47);
- Music makers (page 48);
- Puppet theatre (page 49);
- Convenience food (page 56);
- Carrying sports gear (page 58).

You will find that you need data about 'things' as well as people. You can often make measurements for yourself. Such data is useful but often not as reliable as that in design manuals.

Materials

CHOOSING MATERIALS

One of the most important decisions that you have to make when you are designing is which material to use. Your teacher will sometimes restrict you to only one or two materials but as you become more experienced you will be allowed to choose from a wide range. Asking yourself the following questions about materials will help you to make sensible decisions.

■ WILL IT BE TOO HEAVY?

The density of a material tells you how heavy it will be. A small piece of a very dense material will be very heavy (eg. lead). A large piece of a low density material will be light (eg. expanded polystyrene). Metals are denser than plastics, and plastics are denser than wood. If you think that a material might be too heavy, you have two options: use less of it or use a less dense material instead.

■ WILL IT BE HARD ENOUGH?

Hard materials do not scratch easily. For parts that will take a lot of wear, hardness is important. Metals are harder than plastics which are harder than wood.

■ WILL IT BE STRONG ENOUGH?

The strength of a material tells you how difficult it is to break. Most of the materials in

Same size but different weight

1400 g   100 g

Density

lead   wood

Same size but different stiffness

Stiffness   steel

1 kg

wood

1 kg

Hardness

Saw blades have to be harder than the materials they cut

Conductivity

The metal body lets the heat through but the plastic handle doesn't

Breaking wood – easy; plastic not so easy; metal too difficult for me

Strength

If unprotected, steel rusts and wood rots

school workshops have reasonable strength and are more than strong enough for your designs. The thicker a piece of material is, the stronger it is. Metals are stronger than plastics which are stronger than wood. So if you want to replace a metal part with a wooden part you will almost certainly have to make the wooden part a lot thicker.

■ WILL IT BE STIFF ENOUGH?

A material is stiff if it is difficult to bend. Parts that have to support a lot of weight need to be stiff as well as strong. If they are not stiff they will bend under the load. The thicker a piece of material is the stiffer it is. Metals are stiffer than wood which is stiffer than most plastics. If you decide to replace a metal part with a plastic part you will have to make the plastic part a lot thicker.

■ HOW WILL IT FEEL?

A material that feels cold at room temperature is a good conductor of heat. An insulator (a poor conductor) feels neither hot nor cold at room temperature. Handles are often made from insulators. Metals are good heat conductors; plastic and wood are insulators.

■ DOES IT ROT OR CORRODE?

In ordinary air steel rusts and copper and brass tarnish. This is called *corrosion*. In sea-water they all corrode faster and wood rots. If you use wood or metal in a design you must decide how best to protect them. Most plastic doesn't rot or corrode under any conditions.

WORKING PROPERTIES

When you are deciding which materials to use it is important to keep in mind what you can *do* to the materials you are choosing. If you choose a material that is very difficult to cut or shape, then you could be making life very difficult for yourself. If on the other hand you choose a material that is easy to work, then the making part of your project will go much more smoothly.

You will have worked out which material is the best for your design but you may deliberately choose to use one that is not quite as good but is easier to work. Wood and plastic are easier to cut than metal but they are not as strong or stiff. Wood is lighter than metal or plastic but is very difficult to bend into shape. Metal and plastic are quite easy to bend into shape. Metal or plastic tube might be the lightest and strongest materials for a frame but wooden strip is much easier to join with card corner plates.

Figure 1 *Wood, metal and plastic have distinctive appearances*

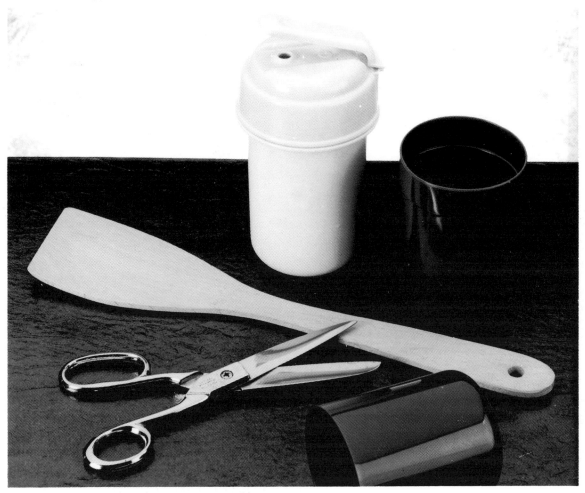

■ WHAT WILL IT LOOK LIKE?

You will want your design to look as attractive as possible and the materials you choose will play a large part in this. You may choose to use the natural appearance of the materials in your design – the shinyness of well finished plastic or the pattern in wood grain. You may choose to cover the material and create a different effect – painting wood or dip coating metal. You will need to think about the appearance that you want right from the beginning.

ACTIVITIES

1 The tumbler in Fig. 1 is plastic. What will it be like made from metal or wood? How will this affect the way it is made and what it is like to use?
2 The cooking spatula in Fig. 1 is wood. What will it be like made from metal or plastic? How will this affect the way it is made? What will it be like to use?
3 The scissors in Fig. 1 are metal. What would they be like made from plastic or wood? How would this affect the way they are made and what they are like to use?

UNDERSTANDING

RESOURCES

WHAT FORM IS IT?

When you choose the material that you are going to use it is important that you think about the form in which the material comes. Most materials can be used in a wide range of forms. It makes sense to choose one that requires the least work. Sometimes you can build up the shape of a part by joining together readily available pieces of material. This is easier than starting with a piece that is too big and removing the parts that you don't need. To be able to think like this you need to know about the forms in which materials come. Pictures on these pages show what is available for wood, metal, plastic, fabric and moulding materials. Sometimes your teacher will restrict you to a particular form of material because this is the best one to use or because that is all that is available. At other times you will have the freedom to choose. Then you can use these pages to help you.

Figure 1 *Metal forms*

Figure 2 *Wood forms*

Figure 3 *A selection of plastic forms*

Figure 4 *Don't forget that fabrics can be useful*

hessian

knitted fabric

linen

printed cotton

felt

Velcro

Figure 5 *Papier maché and clay are easy to use as modelling materials*

ACTIVITIES

For each of the designs in the following projects make out a list of the materials needed and the best form for them to come in:

■ Ronabir's maze game (page 6),
■ Lisa's body adornment (page 10),
■ Annabel's ring can buggy (page 14),
■ Jon's moving toy (page 18),
■ Agnes' moisture sensor (page 26),
■ Julie's windmill (page 30).

Energy

STORING ENERGY

Perhaps the simplest way to store energy is to lift a weight. The weight gains energy as it is lifted and this energy is released as the weight falls. Fig. 1 shows this principle in use. Can you see how the energy stored in the weight is used to drive the pile into the ground? Fig. 2 shows how this same idea can be used to drive a small toy.

Other easy ways to store energy are stretching or twisting rubber bands and stretching or squashing springs. In Fig. 3 the model boats move by using energy stored both in springs and rubber bands. If you need to use a rubber band to store energy you will need to know how long it should be, how thick and how much you need to twist or stretch it. Experiments with different bands will help you to decide.

USING BATTERIES

Batteries are a useful way to store electrical energy. If you want to use a battery to drive a motor or to light a lamp you must choose the right battery for the job. To start with, you need a battery that gives the correct voltage. This will be marked on the case – 1.5 V, 4.5 V, 9 V, 12 V, are all possible. You will need to check with your teacher or a catalogue to find which is the right one. If the voltage is too small the battery will

Figure 1 *Pile driving uses the energy stored in a lifted weight*

Figure 2 *A falling weight makes this toy work*

Figure 3 *Energy stored in springs and rubber bands can work toys*

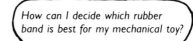

How can I decide which rubber band is best for my mechanical toy?

not give enough energy for the motor to work. If the voltage is too large, the battery will deliver too much energy and the motor could be damaged. When you have chosen the right voltage you will need to decide which type of battery to use. Ever Ready produce a chart to help you. You can use such a chart to decide which battery you would use for:
a ring can buggy, a moisture detector and an electric maze game.

ENERGY MATTERS

In recent years there has been a lot of interest in conserving energy. Fossil fuels will eventually run out and some people think that it is better to use them to make new materials rather than to produce heat. Every material that we use has been produced using energy. So designs that use less material save energy. The posters shown in Fig. 5 have a clear message – waste energy and you waste money.

The use of nuclear energy has always been surrounded by controversy as the headlines in Fig. 6 show. How we choose to use energy in the future is important and you will need to know and understand quite a lot if you are to help make the right decisions. Your work on understanding energy in D and T is just the beginning.

Figure 5 *Energy costs*

Figure 6 *Using nuclear energy is controversial*

FIGHTING FRICTION

Whenever moving parts rub together there is *friction*. Friction creates heat. Energy used up in causing friction is energy wasted. In your designing ensure that parts which move against one another are as smooth as possible and lubricated. Candle wax and talcum powder are good lubricants for wood. Oil is used with metal. Some plastics, e.g. nylon, are self-lubricating.

Fig. 7 shows X-rays of an arthritic hip joint and the plastic and metal joint fitted as a replacement. Can you see where there was friction in the old joint and how it has been removed in the new one?

Look at Julie's windmill on page 30 and Annabel's buggy on page 14. Where would you expect friction to cause difficulties? How would you tackle these problems?

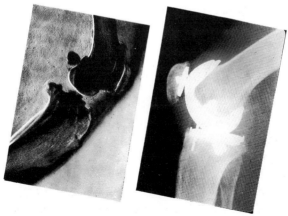

Figure 7 *An arthritic joint (left). Using modern materials to combat arthritis (right)*

RESODURCES

Energy

Ronabir was given the spider toy shown on this page. It contains a small clockwork motor. He was able to understand the energy conversions that were taking place by answering the following questions. Can you?

1 Where does the energy used to wind up the clockwork motor come from?
2 What happens to the spring when the motor is being wound up?
3 How can you tell that the wound up spring has extra energy?
4 Look in the Mechanisms section (page 94) to see why gears are needed.
5 What happens to the spring when the toy is working?
6 What energy form does the toy have as it is moving?
7 Why does the toy eventually stop moving?
8 What has happened to the energy that was stored in the spring?
9 What would happen if you put too much energy in the spring?

Figure 1 *Inside the clockwork motor*

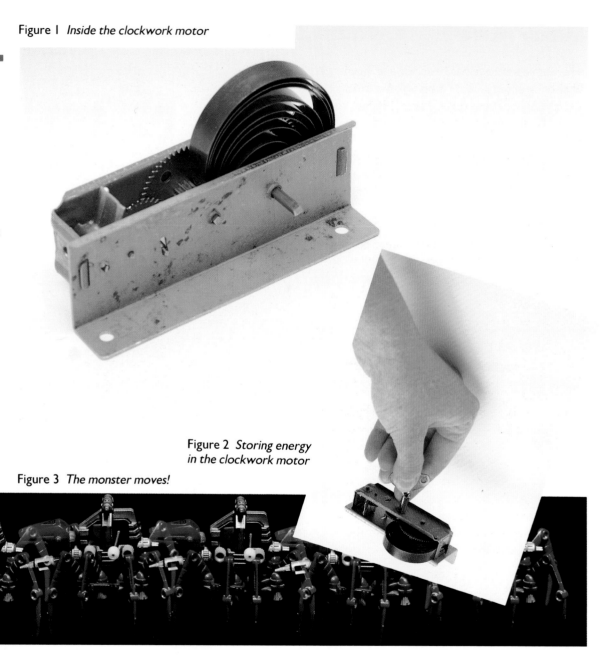

Figure 2 *Storing energy in the clockwork motor*

Figure 3 *The monster moves!*

ENERGY SOURCES

The fossil fuels (coal, oil and natural gas) provide most of the energy that we need in the world at the moment. Some fuels are burned to provide heat directly. Some are burned in internal combustion engines and used for transport. Some are burned in power stations to drive turbines that generate electricity. Nuclear energy from radioactive materials can also be used to generate electricity.

Electricity cannot be stored as electricity, but batteries contain chemicals that can react together to release electrical energy.

Alternative sources of energy are becoming more important – solar energy (energy from sunlight), wind energy, wave energy, tidal energy and geothermal energy (energy from the molten rock beneath the Earth's crust).

Sharon was able to set up the energy conversion system shown here in a science lesson. She was pleased to discover that the work she had done in her D and T lessons helped her understand the way in which the system worked. She could work out which words went in the gaps using some of the following words – heat, light, sound, kinetic, potential, electrical, chemical. Can you? The model shows the stages of producing electric light for most homes. Can you find out the differences from the real system?

I Stored _____ energy in the fuel is converted to _____ by burning.

2 _____ energy is used to boil the water to create steam.

3 Steam is used to give the pistons _____ energy.

4 The pistons transfer their kinetic energy to the flywheel causing it to rotate.

5 The belt driven by the flywheel drives the dynamo.

6 The _____ energy in the dynamo is converted to _____ energy.

7 The bulb converts the electrical energy into _____ and _____.

Energy

HOT AND COLD

The cartons opposite are used to carry food and drink. They keep hot things hot and cold things cold. The materials that they are made of are poor conductors of heat. If hot things are put inside them it takes a long time for the heat to pass through the container to the outside. So the food or drink takes a long time to cool down. If cold things are put in them it takes a long time for heat to pass into the container from the outside. So the food or drink takes a long time to warm up. As heat can pass into or out of the food only through the walls of the carton, the surface area is very important. The best shape will have the least surface area for the greatest volume. This shape is a sphere but it isn't very practical! Can you explain why?

Figure 1 *Fast food containers help stop warming up and cooling down*

ACTIVITIES

1 Use the Materials section to find out which materials are poor conductors of heat.
2 Some hot drink containers have 'turned over' rims. Can you explain why?
3 Make a collection of fast food and drink cartons. Test them out to find the best one.

ENERGY WORK OUT!

Designers use ideas about energy to help them understand how well things work. They can do simple sums to work out how much energy is needed to do certain jobs. This is called *calculating* how much work has to be done. The page opposite shows some examples of these sums and below is an explanation of the information you need.

You need more energy to move a heavy thing than to move a light thing. The weight of the

object needs to be measured in newtons (N). When you weigh something the answer is usually given in kilograms (kg). This is actually the *mass* of the object. It is easy to turn mass into *weight*. A mass of 1 kg is attracted to the Earth with a force of 9.8 N. So you simply multiply the mass of an object (measured in kilograms) by 9.8 (or 10 for rough calculations) to get the weight of the object measured in newtons. The *work done* will also depend on the distance the object has been moved. This *distance* must be measured in metres. The *work done* is calculated by multiplying the weight of the object by the distance it has been moved. So we can write:

Work done = force (N) × distance moved (m).

The answer is in newton metres (Nm). Energy and work done are usually measured in joules (J) and one newton metre is the same as one joule. Joules can be used to measure energy in any form. So heat energy can be measured in joules. Scientists have measured that it takes just over 4 J to raise the temperature of 1 cm³ water by 1°C. It is important to understand the difference between *work done* and *power*. Power is the rate of doing work. To calculate power you will need to know the work done AND the time taken to do it. The time taken is measured in seconds.

Power = work done (Nm or J) ÷ time (s).

The answer is in Nm/s or J/s and these are called watts (W).

UNDERSTANDING

EXAMPLES

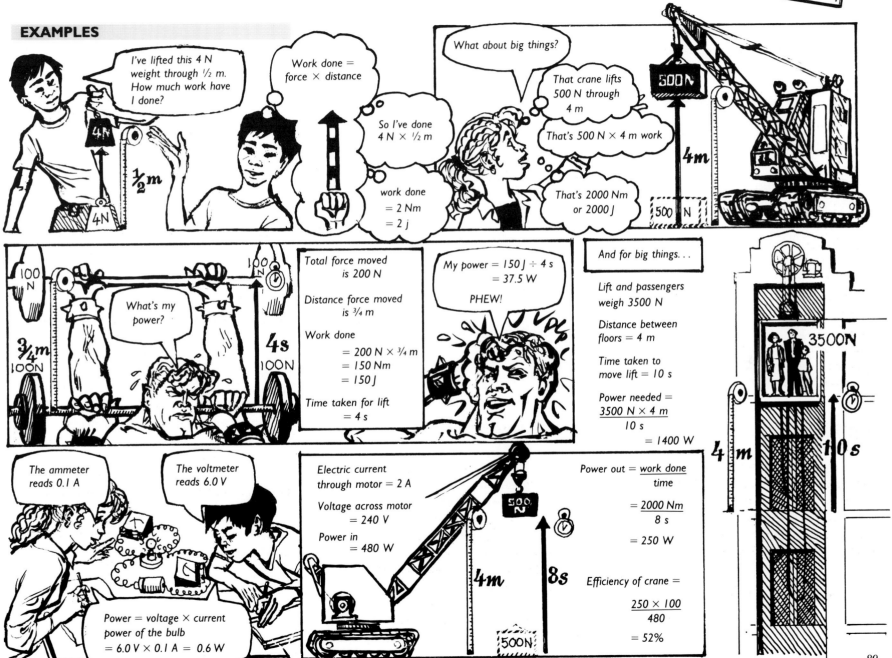

I've lifted this 4 N weight through ½ m. How much work have I done?

Work done = force × distance

So I've done 4 N × ½ m

work done = 2 Nm = 2 J

½m

4N

What about big things?

That crane lifts 500 N through 4 m

That's 500 N × 4 m work

That's 2000 Nm or 2000 J

500N

4m

500 N

What's my power?

¾m

100N

4s

100N

Total force moved is 200 N

Distance force moved is ¾ m

Work done
= 200 N × ¾ m
= 150 Nm
= 150 J

Time taken for lift
= 4 s

My power = 150 J ÷ 4 s = 37.5 W

PHEW!

And for big things...

Lift and passengers weigh 3500 N

Distance between floors = 4 m

Time taken to move lift = 10 s

Power needed =
3500 N × 4 m
—————————
10 s
= 1400 W

3500N

4 m

10 s

The ammeter reads 0.1 A

The voltmeter reads 6.0 V

Power = voltage × current
power of the bulb
= 6.0 V × 0.1 A = 0.6 W

Electric current through motor = 2 A

Voltage across motor = 240 V

Power in = 480 W

500 N

4m

8s

500N

Power out = work done
—————————
time
= 2000 Nm
—————————
8 s
= 250 W

Efficiency of crane =
250 × 100
—————————
480
= 52%

Structures

WHAT IS A STRUCTURE?

A structure is any collection of parts that are joined together so that they support a load. A structure may also enclose a space. So, the following are all structures: buildings of all sorts – churches, houses, flats, mosques, garages, town halls and temples; boats, planes, cars, roads, bridges, large machines such as tower cranes and combine harvesters. And of course the natural world is full of structures – trees, plants, animals, skeletons and shells.

FORCES IN STRUCTURES

It is important for you to understand the forces acting in the different parts of a structure. In this way you will be able to understand how a structure manages to support its load no matter how complicated it seems to be. The structure in Fig. 1 is unusual in that the parts making it up are people! Imagine you are at the bottom. Your body and legs would be being squashed by the weight of those above. These parts of your body are in compression and have to push back against the squashing forces. Your arms linking you to other people are in tension. They have to pull against the stretching forces trying to pull them apart. All the tension and compression forces have to balance out if the structure is to be strong enough. If the person leaning out on the left-hand side was suddenly removed the whole structure would tumble to the ground because the forces were out of balance. When you are trying to understand how a structure works it is worth thinking that you are different parts of the structure. You will find that you can imagine the forces that are acting on you and how you have to respond in order for the structure to support the load.

BEAMS

A basic building block of many structures is the beam. A beam is a length of material that is supported at each end. The load may sit anywhere along the length of the beam. A shelf is a beam. To understand beams it is useful to make a series of beams from A4 sheets of paper. Examples are shown in Fig. 2. The single sheet is very weak and cannot support its own weight. Turning it into corrugated paper makes it stronger and stiffer. Folding and gluing to form a box beam makes it even better. Which of the two boxes in the figure will be best?

COLUMNS

A column is often an important part of structures. Columns have to resist compressive forces. You can find out which is the best shape for a tubular column by making columns from A4 sheets of paper as shown in Fig. 3. Which column do you think will take the greatest load before it crumples?

Figure 1 *The forces in a structure need to balance out*

UNDERSTANDING

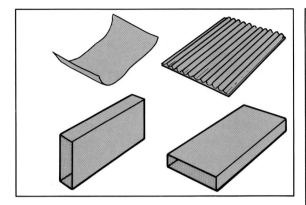

Figure 2 *Exploring designs for beams with paper models*

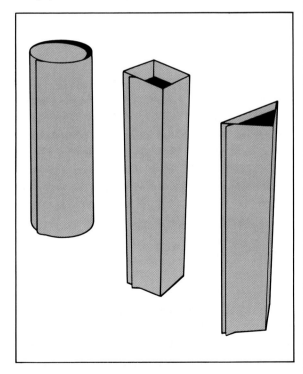

Figure 3 *Exploring designs for columns with paper tubes*

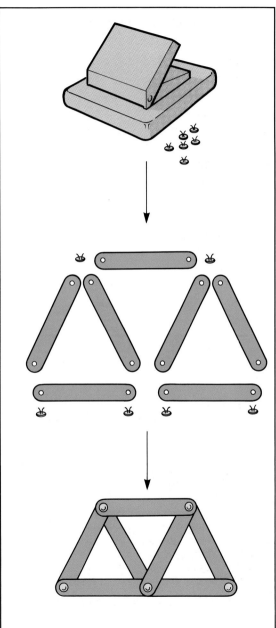

Figure 4 *Exploring framework design*

FRAME WORKS

Many structures are made from frameworks. You can make model frameworks using lolly sticks, a paper punch and paper fasteners as shown in Fig. 4. You use the punch to make holes in the sticks – they split easily when drilled. You use the fasteners to join the sticks together. Frameworks made from linked *triangles* are stiff and strong. They do not change shape easily. Frameworks made from linked *squares* or other shapes change shape easily and are of little use. You will notice that many frameworks have triangles 'built-in' to make sure that the structure works well.

ACTIVITIES

1 Make paper beams from A4 paper as shown in Fig. 2 and find out which is the best box beam.
2 Try making paper tubes of the same diameter but different heights. How does the height of the tube affect its strength?
3 Look at the following projects and decide whether modelling structures with paper or stick will help to develop a good solution.

- Problems with play (page 40),
- Kites and flyers (page 22),
- Puppet theatre (page 49).

Mechanisms

Whenever the way in which an object works involves movement, then there will be *mechanisms* present. So, if you want to design and make things that move or have moving parts you will need to understand mechanisms. A good way to do this is to look at how things with moving parts do actually work.

THE PAPER PUNCH

Fig. I shows a paper punch. You have probably used one just like it. Paper or thin card is slid into position and pushing down on the handle causes two hard metal rods to cut holes. It is important to look closely at exactly how the moving parts are moving. The cross-section drawings in Fig. I help you to do this.

The drawings show the punch handle in the 'ready' position and in the 'just made a hole' position. You should be able to see that the handle has turned (or pivoted) about the point A. The handle is held in place by a rivet at the pivot point. The size of the hole in the handle around this rivet must be just right; too small and the handle will bind on the rivet and be difficult to move, too large and the handle will wobble and not turn as required. The hole needs to be a *sliding* fit around the rivet. The plastic ring pushes down on the cutters. Notice that the cutters move straight up and down, held in an upright position by the guide holes in the framework.

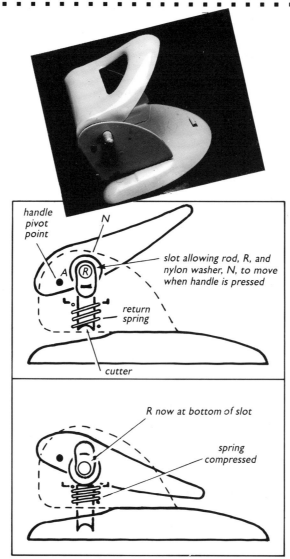

Figure I *Can you spot the moving parts in this hole punch?*

Again, the size of the holes must be just right; too small and the cutters will 'stick', too big and the cutters will not be guided. As with the pivot hole, a sliding fit is needed.

Note that the handle and the plastic ring it pushes do *not* move straight up and down but follow a curved path. The handle does not have to be lifted up into the 'ready' position as the springs around the cutters push it back. So from looking at the paper punch you can see that moving parts may move in a *straight* line or in a *curved* path. You can also see that, whenever a part has to move inside a hole, then a sliding fit is needed.

THE BICYCLE

Fig. 2 shows the chain drive on a bicycle. When you pedal, the crank turns the large toothed wheel. Toothed wheels are called *sprockets*. The piece of metal joining the crank to the sprocket has to fit tightly into both of them. A sliding fit would be of no use. The large sprocket is joined to the small one by a *drive chain*. Both the large and small sprockets rotate when you pedal but the small one goes round faster than the large one. If there are 60 teeth on the large one and 20 on the small one, the small one will move three times faster. Can you work out why?

THE HAND DRILL

When toothed wheels mesh they are called *gears*.

Fig. 3 shows a hand drill. When you use one you notice that the drill bit goes round a lot faster than your turning speed. This is because the drive wheel has a lot more teeth than the driven wheel – as in the bicycle. There is a difference. The plane of the rotary movement has been moved through 90° by using *bevelled gears*.

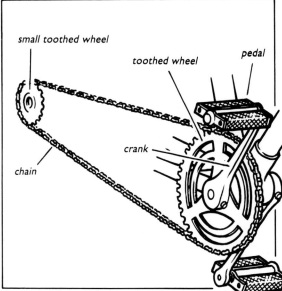

Figure 2 *The mechanism that drives a bicycle*

small toothed wheel

toothed wheel

pedal

crank

chain

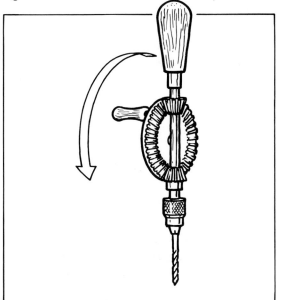

Figure 3 *Gears are needed to work this drill*

THE VACUUM CLEANER

The beater shown in Fig. 4 is used to brush out the dust as the cleaner moves along. It needs to rotate quite slowly. It is driven by means of a belt which connects it to the drive shaft of the motor. This shaft is narrower than the beater. This causes the beater to rotate more slowly than the drive shaft. Can you explain why?

THE TUMBLE DRIER

The belt drive used in the tumble drier shown in Fig. 5 has to make the containing drum spin much more slowly than the drive shaft of the electric motor. This is achieved by using a small *pulley* on the drive shaft and a much larger pulley on the drum.

If you get the chance to look at the belt drive in a vacuum cleaner or the inside of a tumble drier, you might find that the belt has 'teeth' which fit into grooves on the pulley wheels. What advantage over a smooth belt does this arrangement have?

Figure 4 *Can you see why the beater goes more slowly than the motor?*

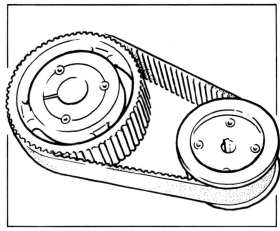

Figure 5 *What would happen if a large drive pulley was used?*

ACTIVITIES

You will find it useful to look at the following items to find out how they work:

sewing machine, food mixer, electric drill, record player, tape player.

If possible it is worth taking off any coverplates so that you can see the working parts. You can also learn a lot by taking the working parts to pieces *and* putting them back together again. If you try this make sure that you have permission, that they are not plugged in and that the item is not a prize possession.

Look in Resources for Drawing and Modelling to find out how to model simple mechanisms. Try to produce working models of the items you investigated.

LEVERS

The handle on the paper punch on page 92 is an example of a *lever*. You apply a force to the handle. This is called the *effort*. It makes the lever turn about the pivot point and apply a force onto the cutters. This is called the *load*. The punch is shown as a simple line diagram in Fig. I(a). Because the load is nearer the pivot point than the effort, the force of the load is greater than the force of the effort. Using a lever like this will always make a job easier. It is called a *force multiplier*. Notice that the distance through which the effort force moves is larger than the distance through which the load moves.

Fig. I(b) shows another sort of lever. The effort, load and pivot point are marked. Will this lever multiply force? Can you find this lever in a pair of pliers?

The lever shown in Fig. I(c) is not a force multiplier. Here the distance moved by the load is greater than the distance moved by the effort. You can find out how to make models of simple levers on page 119.

GEARS

You can change the speed and direction of *rotary* movement using gears. A simple gear train is shown in Fig. 2. Note that the speed of the driven gear will depend on how many teeth it has compared with the driver gear. If it has more teeth it will go slower. If it has fewer teeth it will go faster. Note also that the driven gear rotates in the *opposite* direction to the driver gear. If you want to change the speed by a lot then you will need to use a compound gear train as shown in Fig. 3. Here a small drive gear drives a large gear. A small gear on the same axle as the large gear drives a large gear on a separate axle.

CAMS

You can use cams to change rotary movement into straight line movement. When the cams shown in Fig. 4 turn they cause the rods resting on them to move up and down. The exact nature of this movement will depend on the shape of the cam. The cam on the right causes a gentle rise and a sudden drop. What about the others?

Figure 2 *A simple gear train*

Figure 3 *A compound gear train*

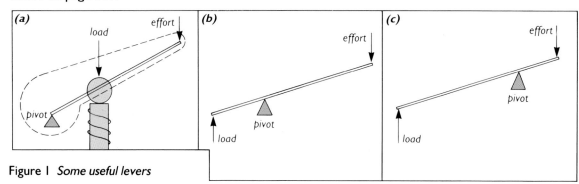

Figure 1 *Some useful levers*

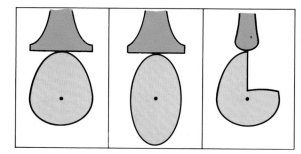

Figure 4 *Can you see how the followers will move for each cam?*

LINKAGES

You can connect levers together to form *linkages*. You can use linkages to make things move in a particular direction. Look at the linkages shown in Fig. 5. Try to work out the direction of the output movement for the given input. Will it be in a different direction? Will it be bigger or smaller?

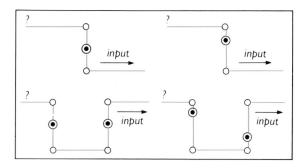

Figure 5 *How will the output motions differ from the input in these linkages?*

CRANKS AND SLIDERS

A *crank* is a lever that turns in a circle. So the pedal on a bicycle is a crank. The longer the crank the more force it applies. You can join a crank to a slider by a linkage called a connecting (*con*) rod.

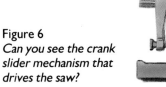

Figure 6
Can you see the crank slider mechanism that drives the saw?

Figure 7 *There is always a lot to see in a mechanical toy*

The con rod must be free to pivot where it joins both the crank and the slider. For every turn of the crank the slider will move forwards and backwards. This mechanism is used in mechanical hacksaws, (Fig. 6).

LOOKING TO LEARN

You can find out a lot about mechanisms by looking at simple toys that have moving parts. The clockwork 'bird' shown in Fig. 7 has a simple gear train driving the wheels and a cam for flapping the wings. How would you change the gear train to increase the toy's speed? How could you change the cam to cause the wings to make a smaller flap, to make a bigger flap, to make alternate big and small flaps or to flap more often?

DESIGNING MECHANISMS

There are several important things to think about. You must be clear about what the input motion is. You must describe it precisely – is it straight line, or turning or rotating? Is it fast or slow? You also need to decide how this motion will be achieved – a hand turning a handle, a clockwork or electric motor, a syringe pushing a lever; there are lots of possibilities.

Next you must be clear about the output motion that you want. You must describe it precisely. You need to compare the input and output motions so that you know the changes in speed, direction and size that you have to achieve.

Now you can review the mechanisms you know about and decide which ones will do the trick. You may need to choose between different possibilities. The simplest one, that is easiest to make and which has the least chance of going wrong, is the best bet. It is worth modelling the mechanism to check that it does work. Jon did this for his moving toy on page 20.

Pneumatics

Compressed air is air that has been forced into a small space. You compress air every time you blow up a balloon or pump up a bicycle tyre. This is hard work, and in industry machines called compressors are used. They can be operated by electricity or diesel fuel. Any machine that uses compressed air to do work is called a *pneumatic system*.

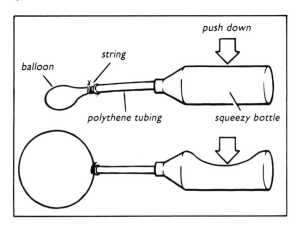

Figure I *Simple pneumatics to blow up a balloon*

You can make a simple pneumatic system as shown in Fig. 1. When you press on the squeezy bottle, air is forced into the balloon and makes it inflate. The more air you can squeeze out of the bottle the more air is forced into the balloon and the more it inflates. It is important that there are no leaks in your system. When you squeeze the bottle the air will always take the easiest path. So escaping through a hole, however small, will be

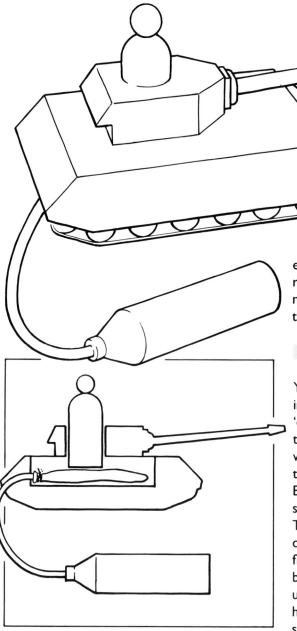

Figure 2 *Simple pneumatics used in a toy tank*

easier than blowing up the balloon. For this reason you will need to make sure that there are no leaks where the tubing joins to the bottle and the balloon.

DESIGNING PNEUMATIC TOYS

You can use a simple pneumatic system to add interest to a child's toy, as shown in Fig. 2. The 'driver' of the tank can be made to look out of the turret by inflating the balloon inside the tank with the squeezy bottle. If you decide to make a toy like this you will need to plan it carefully. Balloons wear out and can leak, so your design should allow the balloon to be changed easily. The plastic tubing should fit into the toy so that it doesn't spoil the overall appearance. The pop-up figure should not be too heavy otherwise the balloon will not be able to lift it. You will need to use light materials, and perhaps design it to be hollow. It will also be important to decorate the squeezy bottle so that it looks as though it belongs with the toy.

HOW MUCH WILL IT LIFT?

You can find out how much your squeezy bottle and balloon arrangement will lift as follows. Arrange the balloon so that it can lift a thin piece of card. This gives a flat surface for weights, (Fig. 3). Place a 100g mass on the card and see if squeezing the bottle causes the weight to rise. Carefully add more weights until you reach a point where, no matter how hard you squeeze, the weights don't rise.

At this stage it is easier to squash the air into the existing space than inflate the balloon. The weight that can only just be lifted is the most that your pneumatic system will lift. You can then work out the pressure in your system by dividing the maximum weight lifted (measured in newtons) by the area of the card (measured in square metres). The result will be in newtons per square metre (sometimes called pascals).

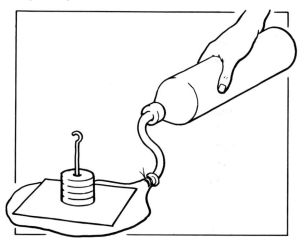

Figure 3 *How much will it lift?*

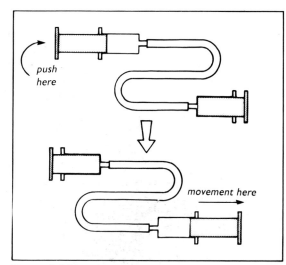

Figure 4 *Using syringes*

USING SYRINGES

You can also use syringes, joined by plastic tubing, to make a simple pneumatic system. One syringe with the plunger pulled out (full of air) is joined by the tubing to another syringe with the plunger pushed in (empty of air). Pushing the 'out' plunger in makes the air trapped in the system force the 'in' plunger out. In this way movement can be transmitted around corners or wherever the plastic joining tube can go.

You will find that the response of this system is slow. There is a slight lag between when the 'out' plunger is pushed in and the 'in' plunger starts to move. This is because the air in the syringe has to be compressed a little before there is enough pressure to overcome the resistance to movement of the 'in' plunger.

PNEUMATIC PUPPETS

You can use both syringes and balloons to add interesting and unusual features to puppets as shown in Fig. 5. If you choose to do this, you will have to plan your design so that the pneumatic system does not interfere with the way the puppet is moved by the puppeteer.

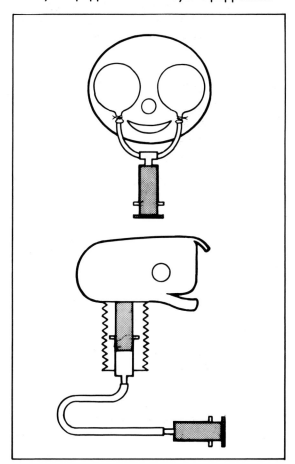

Figure 5 *Special effects puppets with pneumatic controls*

Hydraulics

You can overcome the time lag of the simple air-filled syringe system by filling the syringes and connecting tubing with *water*. Because water is incompressible, any push or pull at one syringe is immediately transmitted to the other syringe. Any air bubbles trapped in the system give a time lag so it is important to completely fill the system with water. You can do this by using a bowl of water as shown in Fig. 1. Any machine that uses a liquid to transmit force from one place to another is called a *hydraulic system*. The digging and earth-moving equipment on the JCB shown in Fig. 2 is powered by a hydraulic system.

Figure 1 *Filling the syringes and tubing with water*

Figure 2 *Heavy machinery uses hydraulic control*

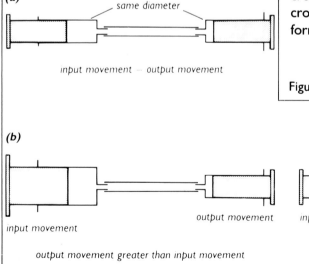

(a)

same diameter

input movement — output movement

(b)

input movement

output movement

output movement greater than input movement

input movement

output movement

output movement smaller than input movement

CHOOSING SYRINGES

You can design your hydraulic system to produce a different range of output movements for a given input. You do this by choosing different syringes as shown in Fig. 3. If both input and output syringes have the same cross-section then the movement of the output plunger will be the *same* as that of the input plunger. If the input syringe has a larger cross-sectional area than the output syringe then any movement of the input plunger will give a *larger* movement of the output plunger. So, if the input syringe has a smaller cross-sectional area than the output syringe then any movement of the input plunger will give a *smaller* movement of the output plunger. You can investigate this effect for yourself quite easily. Use the results of any investigation to work out why changing the cross-sectional area has this effect. Note that the cross-sectional area of the syringe is given by the formula πr^2, where r is the radius of the syringe.

Figure 3 *Input and output with different syringe sizes*

HYDRAULIC ROBOT ARM

You can design and make a robot arm that is powered by syringes filled with water. An outline design is shown in Fig. 4. The way it works is clear. Syringe 1 moves the lower part. Syringe 2 moves the upper part. Syringe 3 operates the gripper. There is a pivot point, A, between the base and the lower part. There is another pivot point, B, between the upper and lower parts. The design is far from complete and you will need to think about the following points:

■ Exactly where will you attach the syringes?
■ How will you attach the plungers? They might need to pivot.
■ How will you attach the bodies of the syringes? They might need to pivot.
■ The flexible tubing connecting the syringes will need to be kept tidy and must not interfere with the movement of the arm.
■ The user must be able to tell what each syringe does. You might colour code them by filling each with a different coloured water. You might need to design a control panel.

Three of the many possibilities for the design of the gripper are shown in Fig. 5. In diagram (a), one jaw moves and it is held open by a small spring. The syringe plunger closes the jaw by pushing on a lever. In (b), only one jaw moves but it is held closed by a small spring. The syringe plunger opens the jaw by pushing on a lever. The plunger is not attached to the lever in either of these designs. In (c), both jaws move and are held

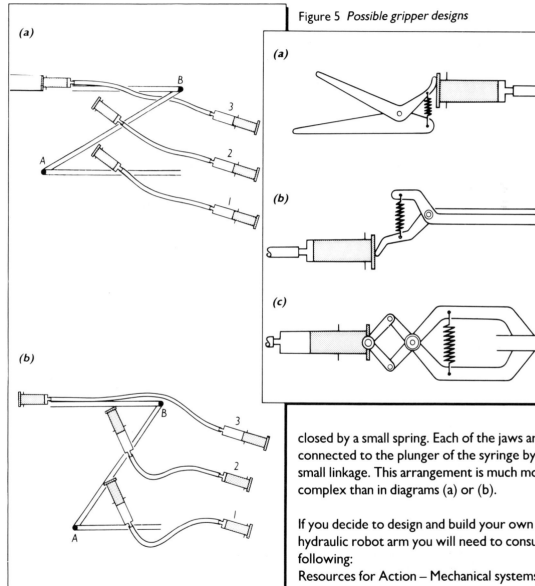

Figure 5 *Possible gripper designs*

Figure 4 *The beginnings of a robot arm*

closed by a small spring. Each of the jaws are connected to the plunger of the syringe by a small linkage. This arrangement is much more complex than in diagrams (a) or (b).

If you decide to design and build your own hydraulic robot arm you will need to consult the following:
Resources for Action – Mechanical systems and Flexible joints, pages 120 and 119;
Resources for Understanding – Levers, Linkages and Designing mechanisms, pages 94 and 95.

RESESOURCES
[UNDERSTANDING]

Electricity and electronics

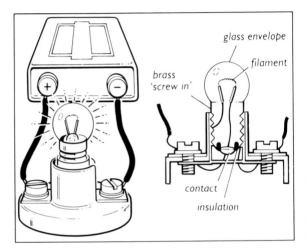

Figure 1 *Lighting a bulb with a battery
Inside the bulb and holder*

glass envelope
filament
brass 'screw in'
contact
insulation

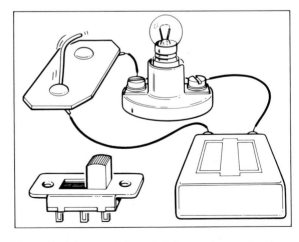

Figure 2 *A home-made switch from wire, card and
paper fasteners with the 'bought-in' version*

LIGHTING A BULB

It is easy to light a bulb using a battery. You connect wires from the positive and negative terminals of the battery to the terminals of the bulb holder as shown in Fig. 1. The bulb lights up because the battery pushes electricity through the thin filament in the bulb, heating it up and making it glow brightly. The bulb holder is designed so that it connects one terminal of the battery to each end of the filament.

USING A SWITCH

In this arrangement the bulb is always on, but what if you want to turn it off sometimes? With a simple switch you can do this easily. You can make a simple switch using card, wire and paper fasteners as Fig. 2 shows. By moving the wire 'joiner' you can break the path of the electricity. The battery cannot push electricity across this gap so the electric current will not flow through the bulb. To switch the bulb on, you close the gap with the wire joiner. The bought in switch also shown in Fig. 2 does the same job. It 'clicks' when it is moved from the *off* to the *on* position and it will last a lot longer.

DESCRIBING AN ELECTRICAL CIRCUIT

The best way to describe an electrical circuit is to draw a *circuit diagram*. Each electrical part has its own symbol which is easy to draw. The circuit diagram for a bulb, battery and switch circuit is shown in Fig. 3.

The battery symbol is
The wire symbol is
The bulb symbol is

Can you work out the symbol for a simple switch? This kind of switch is called a *single pole, single throw* switch.

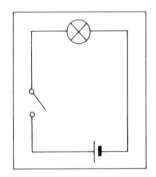 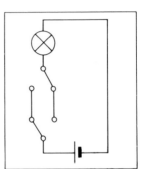

Figure 3 *Circuit diagram for the bulb, battery and switch circuit*   Figure 4 *A two way switching circuit*

The circuit diagram for a two way light circuit is shown in Fig. 4. Here the switch design is different from the simple switch. It is called a *single pole, double throw* switch. Can you see how it is possible to switch the light bulb on and off from either of the switches? Can you think where this lighting circuit is used in your home?

ACTIVITIES

Using card, wire and paper fasteners make two single pole, double throw switches and connect them to a battery and bulb so that you have the two way light circuit.

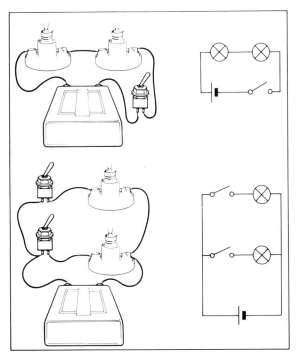

Figure 5 *Two bulbs in series (top)*
Two bulbs in parallel (bottom)

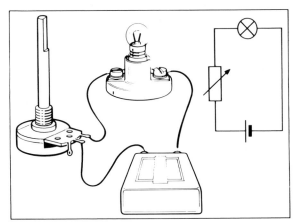

Figure 6 *Controlling the brightness of a bulb*

■ SERIES AND PARALLEL

The circuits in Fig. 5 each have two bulbs. In the first circuit they are in line with each other. The same electric current has to flow through both bulbs. These bulbs are in series. In the second circuit the electric current has a choice of two paths. It divides into two and some of the current flows through each bulb. You can switch off the current to one of the bulbs and still leave the other path open so that the bulb stays 'on'. In this circuit the bulbs are in parallel.

■ VARIABLE BRIGHTNESS

You can reduce the brightness of the bulb in a simple circuit by decreasing the current flowing through the bulb. Fig. 6 shows how you can arrange the circuit with a variable resistor (or potentiometer) to vary the brightness of the bulb. The variable resistor is put in series with the bulb. It resists (or slows down) the flow of current. It is connected using the middle tag and one of the outside tags. The brightness of the bulb can then be adjusted by turning the central knob.

■ LIGHT-EMITTING DIODES

As a bulb needs a lot of current to keep it glowing it is sometimes worth using a light-emitting diode (an LED) instead. These need a small current. They give out light only if they are wired into the circuit the right way round and each one needs a fixed value resistor to protect it from too great a current. LEDs come in three colours (red, green and yellow)

Figure 7 *Protecting an LED with a resistor*

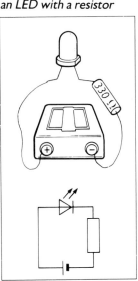

but they do not give a lot of light. They are often used as warning or indicator 'lamps' in electronic circuits. Fig. 7 shows how to wire an LED plus resistor into a circuit, and their circuit symbols.

■ THE RESISTOR COLOUR CODE

Fixed value resistors have a series of coloured stripes on them which show how many *ohms* (or how big) their resistance is. The silver or gold stripe must always be on the right-hand side when you are reading the value of the other stripes from left to right. Fig. 8 shows you how to turn the coloured stripes into numbers of ohms. The symbol for ohms is Ω, and for a large value resistor such as $10\ 000\ \Omega$, you can write $10\ k\Omega$, where k stands for $\times 1000$.

first number	second number	silver or gold

number of zeros

Black 0	Green 5
Brown 1	Blue 6
Red 2	Purple 7
Orange 3	Grey 8
Yellow 4	White 9

Figure 8 *The resistor colour code*

Electricity and electronics

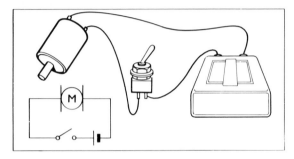

Figure 1 *Connecting a motor to a battery, and the circuit diagram*

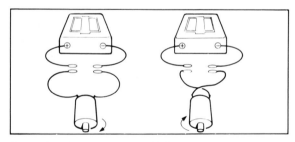

Figure 2 *How to reverse a DC motor*

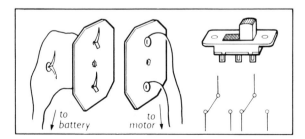

Figure 3 *A home-made reversing switch, the bought-in version and the circuit symbol*

USING MOTORS

A DC electric motor can be wired into a circuit in the same way as a light bulb. As with a light bulb, a simple single pole, single throw switch will allow you to turn it on and off. What if you want to change the direction in which the motor is turning? You can't use a simple switch because you need to reverse the direction of the electric current through the motor. There is a switch which will do this. It is called a *double pole, double throw* switch. Fig. 3 shows you how to make one from card and paper fasteners. Can you see that turning the card discs reverses the battery connections to the motor?

It is possible to buy switches that can be used to reverse DC motors. The one shown in Fig. 3 is a slide switch with a neutral position in the middle. Careful wiring is needed to ensure that the slide switch will reverse the motor. Can you see how to do it from the circuit diagram?

ACTIVITIES

Make a card reversing switch and test it out.

There are many types of switch besides the simple switch. You will need to decide which one is the best for your circuit.

■ MEMBRANE PANEL SWITCHES

This is one of the simplest switches. It can also be used as a pressure pad in an alarm system. Exactly how to make one is described in Fig. 4.

Note that it is only 'on' while it is being pressed. As soon as the pressure is released it turns 'off'.

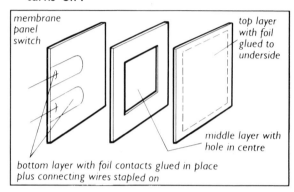

Figure 4 *How to make a membrane panel switch*

■ REED SWITCHES

A reed switch is a switch that is operated by a magnet. It is turned on when a magnet is put next to it. This switch is often used in security systems to guard windows and doors. The switch is built into the frame and the magnet into the door or window. If either is opened, then the switch is turned off and this can be used to set off an alarm. Fig. 5 shows a reed switch and its circuit symbol.

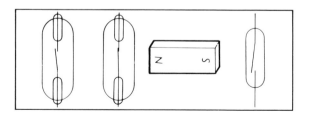

Figure 5 *A reed switch is turned on by a magnet The symbol for a reed switch*

SENSORS

It is useful to be able to detect when the temperature drops in a greenhouse and to respond by turning on a heater. The first stage in this process is to *sense* the change in temperature. There are a range of 'sensors' which can detect different changes in the environment (such as an increase in temperature). Those which you will probably use work by having a resistance which changes as the environment changes. Several sensors and their symbols are shown in Fig. 6. The *light dependent resistor* (LDR) has a high resistance in the dark but a low resistance in the light. The *thermistor* has a low resistance when it is warm but a high resistance when it is cold. The *water probes* have a high resistance when there is air in the gap but a lower one when this is bridged by water. The *tilt switch* which can be used to detect deviation from horizontal level works in a similar way: the mercury which bridges the gap between the probes has a low resistance. When the switch is tilted far enough, the gap is not bridged and the resistance between the probes rises.

TRANSISTORS

The transistor is a switch with no moving parts. This means that it can switch on and off very quickly and it doesn't wear out like mechanical switches. The sort of transistor that you are likely to use is shown in Fig. 7. It is an 'npn' type. It has three legs to which connections are made. These legs have special names: *base*, *collector* and *emitter*. It is important to know which leg is

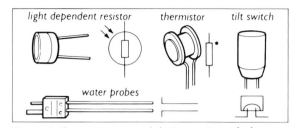

Figure 6 *Some sensors and their circuit symbols*

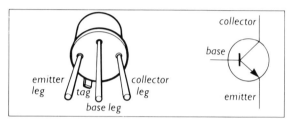

Figure 7 *An npn transistor and circuit symbol*

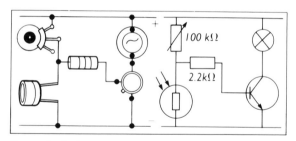

Figure 8 *A photo switch circuit using one npn transistor*

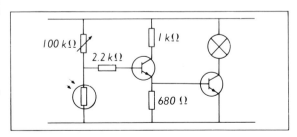

Figure 9 *A better photoswitch using the Darlington pair arrangement of two transistors*

which and Fig. 7 will help you. To turn on the transistor, a small current has to enter the *base* leg. Only then will a current be able to flow from the *collector* to the *emitter*. If there is no current entering the base of the transistor then the transistor is switched off. A small current into the base of the transistor lets a large current flow through the transistor so in addition to being a switch the transistor is also acting as an *amplifier* (as a small current results in a larger one).

THE PHOTOSWITCH CIRCUIT

The circuit shown in Fig. 8 uses an LDR as a sensor and a single transistor to light a bulb when the LDR is put in the dark. It works like this: the battery is trying to push electricity from the positive rail across the circuit to the negative rail. When the LDR is in the light the electricity takes the easy route through the $100\,k\Omega$ variable resistor and the LDR. When the LDR is in the dark its resistance rises and some electricity flows through the $2.2\,k\Omega$ fixed resistor and into the base of the transistor. This turns the transistor on and electricity can now flow through the transistor via the collector and the emitter causing the bulb to light up.

You can make a better photoswitch by using two transistors instead of one. This arrangement of transistors is called a *Darlington pair* and this circuit is shown in Fig. 9. It can be used with heat, water and tilt sensors as well as a light sensor. The circuit can also drive a small buzzer if a sound alarm is required.

Electricity and electronics

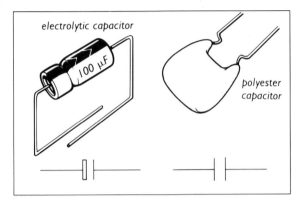

Figure 1 *Capacitors and their circuit symbols*

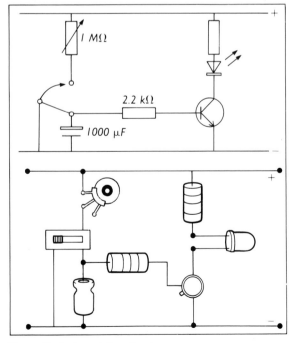

Figure 2 *A time delay circuit*

TIME DELAY CIRCUITS

Capacitors store electricity. How much they can store is measured in microfarads (μF). Fig. 1 shows two sorts of capacitor with their circuit symbols. *Polyester* capacitors store only tiny amounts of electricity and can be connected into a circuit either way round. *Electrolytic* capacitors store more electricity but they must be connected into the circuit the correct way round.

Capacitors take time to store electricity, so they can be used to make time delay circuits. When the switch is moved to the 'on' position in the circuit in Fig. 2, the electricity flows into the capacitor via the variable resistor. The time which the capacitor takes to fill up with electricity depends on how fast electricity can flow into it. This will depend on the setting of the resistor. It will take longer with a large resistance than with a small one. When the capacitor becomes full, electricity will then flow into the base of the transistor. This turns it on so that the LED comes on. The delay between the circuit being switched on and the LED lighting up depends on the size of the capacitor and the resistance from the variable resistor.

CIRCUITS THAT FLASH LIGHTS AND MAKE NOISE

The circuit shown in Fig. 3 uses the time delays provided by two capacitors to flash lights on and off alternately. The timing of the flashes is controlled by the sizes of the capacitors and the

resistors in the circuit. For example, large electrolytic capacitors fed via large resistors give long flashes. You can use small value polyester capacitors to flash the lights so fast it looks like they are on all the time.

Then if you use a speaker instead of a light bulb the circuit makes a noise, (Fig. 4).

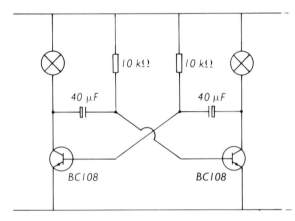

Figure 3 *Flashing light circuit*

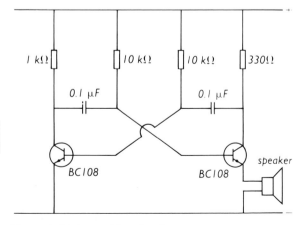

Figure 4 *Noise-making circuit*

INTRODUCING MICROCHIPS

To make electronic circuits smaller and easier to use, designers developed *chips* in which lots of separate components are linked together in circuits that are much too small to see. Chips are called integrated circuits (ICs).

Fig. 5 shows a chip, and the circuits inside viewed through a microscope. Connections are made to the circuits inside the chip through its metal legs or *pins*. It is important that you connect any additional components to the correct pins, otherwise the chip will not work properly and it may be damaged. The best way to try out a circuit is to use a breadboard. The chip and any other components can be 'plugged in' without any soldering.

The circuits described here use a useful chip called a 556 Timer.

■ THE MONOSTABLE CIRCUIT

This circuit (shown in Fig. 6) gives an output for a set time from a single brief input. The length of this time depends on the size of the resistors and capacitors connected to the chip. This circuit can be used to light LEDs or sound buzzers in steady-hand games where the input is a very brief contact. It can also be used to drive motors for a set period in toys.

■ THE ELECTRIC ORGAN

The circuit diagram and breadboard layout are shown in Fig. 7. The circuits in the chip behave like the noise-making circuit in Fig. 4. The pitch of the sound is set by the resistors.

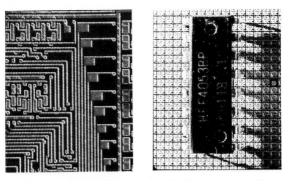

Figure 5 *The integrated circuit (left) is much smaller than its plastic case and connecting legs (right)*

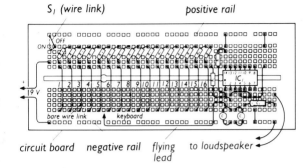

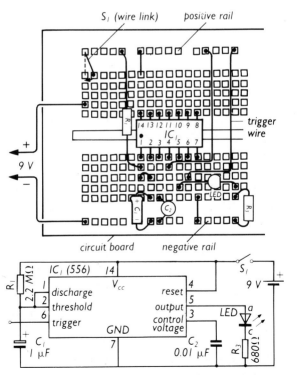

Figure 6 *Circuit diagram and breadboard layout for a monostable circuit*

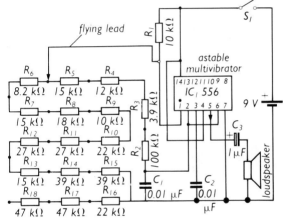

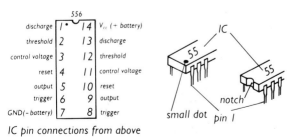

IC pin connections from above

Figure 7 *Circuit and layout diagrams for an electric organ*

Computers

Most schools have microcomputers and you will probably be able to use these in a variety of lessons including D and T. You do not have to understand how the computer works 'inside' in order to use it. You *do* need to know how to operate the software that gives the computer its instructions. This usually comes on a *disc*. The disc drive that is attached to the computer sends instructions from the disc to the computer. Some software comes in the form of a microchip which can be plugged directly into the computer.

You will need to become familiar with any software you use so that you learn how to get the best out of it. All it takes is a little practice. Much of the software now available in schools is very 'user friendly' so half an hour's practice is often all you need to become good at using it. It helps if you work with friends.

WORD PROCESSING

Whenever you have to produce a written account it is worth considering using a computer as a word processor. Once you have 'written' your account on the screen you can go through it and correct mistakes or change anything that isn't quite right. This is called *editing*. It is much easier to edit 'on screen' than to produce several rough drafts. Once the writing is as you want it you can store it on disc. You can also connect the computer to a printer and print it out. Most

Figure 1 *Word processing helps you produce professional reports for your design folder*

Figure 2 *Image processing helps you get the design you want*

word processing software allows you to change the size and style of the printing. Spelling check programmes are also available. This enables you to produce a design folder that is clearly laid out and easy to read, however bad your handwriting.

IMAGE PROCESSING

Just as you can use software to produce and edit text so you can use design software to generate images on the screen. This often involves using a *mouse* as well as the keyboard. As with word processing you can easily change what's on the screen until you are satisfied.

With the simplest software you can draw and colour in on the screen. The image can be stored on disc and also printed out. This sort of software is useful when you are trying to think up and develop ideas. The results can be included in your design folder. Slightly more complex software allows you to manipulate the image you have drawn. Mirror images, simple rotations, squashing, stretching, magnifying, are all possible.

It is easy to build up a library of shapes stored on disc and then to call up the ones that you want as you need them. This saves redrawing. Such software is useful for drawing circuit diagrams and plans of things you want to make. Print outs of these can be included in your design folder. More complex software enables you to design 3D objects on the screen but it does take longer to learn how to use these programmes.

DATABASES

It is possible to store large amounts of information on a disc. It is also possible to organise this information so that it is easy to get at. These are the main ideas behind a *database*. A database on the properties of materials will be useful because it will contain most of the information you need to help you decide on exactly which material to choose. The information on such a database will cover that stored in many books. Providing you have learned how to use the database, it will save you hours of looking things up. In fact, using a database is simply a new and more powerful way to look things up. The particular pieces of information that you need can usually be printed out so that you can present them in your design folder as part of your 'finding out'.

Figure 3 *A database gives quick access to a lot of information*

Figure 4 *Computer Aided Design in use in industry*

SIMULATIONS

Software that models the behaviour of the real world is very useful for designers. It is possible to model the behaviour of an electrical circuit that you have designed so that you can check out whether it will work or not *before* you solder the components together. This can avoid costly mistakes as well as teaching you a lot about electronics. Industrial designers and engineers use such software to model the performance of new designs of cars and aeroplanes. In this way expensive failures get no further than the drawing board.

CONTROL

You can use a computer to control simple machines – a buggy or a robot arm. You will probably use a control programme into which you type the instructions you want the machine to obey. The computer will then transmit these instructions to the machine via an interface. All the computer is doing is turning motors on and off according to your instructions. It is possible to use sensors to feed information to the computer. The computer can then be programmed to respond to this information in a particular way. In this way you can use two light sensors to control the motors driving a buggy so that it follows a dark line on the floor. Any programmes you have written can be printed out and included in your design folder.

Figure 5 *You can use a computer to control models you have designed*

Marking out

■ WHICH MARKER?

To begin with, you have to decide which marker to use. This will depend on the material you are trying to mark. Different materials need different markers. For marking wood across the grain use a marking knife or pencil. For plastic use a spirit-based felt-tip pen or a chinagraph pencil. If the plastic still has a protective paper covering you can use an ordinary pencil. For most metals use a scriber, although you can use pencil on aluminium.

■ CHECK FOR A STRAIGHT EDGE

In most cases you will need to mark out from a straight edge. You can test for this using a steel rule as shown in Fig. 3.

■ MARKING STRAIGHT LINES

To mark lines at right angles to a straight edge use a try square, (Fig. 4). There are different try squares for wood and metal. Use the metal ones for plastic. To mark lines parallel to a straight edge there are different tools for wood and metal. For metal use odd-leg callipers, (Fig. 2). For wood use a marking gauge, (Fig. 5).

■ MARKING CURVES

If you want to mark circles or radius curves on wood you can use a pencil compass. For metal or plastic use a pair of dividers, (Fig. 6).

△ Figure 1 *Markers*

▽ Figure 2 *Using odd leg callipers*

△ Figure 3 *Using a straight edge*

▽ Figure 4 *Using a try square*

△ Figure 5 *Using a marking gauge*

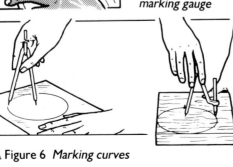
△ Figure 6 *Marking curves*

■ MARKING ODD SHAPES

You can mark out irregular shapes by using a template, as shown in Fig. 7. The marker simply follows the line of the cut out. If you only need one shape this can be made from paper and stuck to the material. Where the shape has to be repeated a template made from stiff card is better.

△ Figure 7 *Using templates*

Practical hints

1. Always check your marking out before you cut the material.
2. Mark out your material so that you waste as little as possible.

ACTIVITIES

Use flow charts to show how you would tackle the marking out in the following projects:

■ cams for a mechanical toy (see page 20);
■ sides for a wooden pencil box (see page 36);
■ thin plywood blades for a model windmill (see page 30);
■ sheet metal probes for a moisture detector (see page 26);
■ the clear acrylic cover of a maze game (see page 9);
■ sheet metal 'petals' for a flower-design brooch (see page 12);

Cutting

■ WHICH TOOL?

Exactly which cutting tool you choose to use will depend on the material you are cutting – wood, plastic or metal; and whether you want to cut a straight line or a curve.

■ HOLDING THE MATERIAL

Whatever material you are cutting it is important to hold it firmly. You may do this by hand on a sawing board for small pieces of wood, but often you will need to grip the material firmly by using a vice or a G clamp.

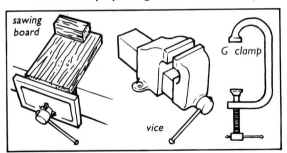

△ Figure 8 *Tools for holding material*

■ CUTTING WOOD

The *tenon saw* is a useful general purpose saw for cutting wooden strips to length and for cutting *straight-sided* shapes from plywood and hardboard sheet.

You can use a *coping saw* to cut *curves* in wood. The blade is very thin and it can be twisted to allow the frame to clear the piece of wood.

■ CUTTING METAL

You can cut tube, rod and bar to the length you need using a *hacksaw*. Hacksaws come in two sizes – the small, 'junior' hacksaw and a larger version. You can use *tinsnips* for cutting out shapes from sheet metal. There are two types: those with straight blades for cutting straight lines and those with curved blades for cutting curves. You can hold the tinsnips in the vice and push down to get extra pressure.

■ CUTTING PLASTIC

You can cut straight lines in soft plastic sheet using a sharp knife and a ruler. Curved lines may be cut using tinsnips. For harder plastic sheet, such as acrylic, you will need to use a hacksaw for straight lines or an abrafile for curves. An abrafile is like a coping saw but the blade cuts in any direction.

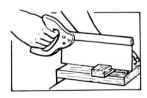

◁ Figure 9 *Using a tenon saw to cut straight lines in softwood*

▽ Figure 10 *Using a coping saw to cut curves in plywood*

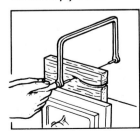

△ Figure 11 *Using a hacksaw to cut straight through metal tube*

▽ Figure 12 *Using tinsnips to cut metal sheet*

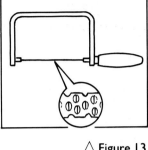

△ Figure 13 *The abrafile*

Practical hints

1. To stop your work from vibrating, hold it close to where you will cut.
2. If you are using a vice or clamp protect your material with pieces of scrap wood.
3. Always saw slowly to one side of the line, into waste material.

ACTIVITIES

Use the information on this page to decide which tool you would use for the following cutting jobs:

■ cutting out aluminium sheet to be used for a body shell in a ring can buggy (see page 17);
■ cutting out geometric shapes from acrylic sheet for parts of a brooch (see page 12);
■ cutting out a face shape from plywood for use in a mechanical toy (see page 20);
■ cutting a wooden block to be used as a base for a moisture sensor (see page 28).

Drilling

Whenever you want to make a circular hole you will need to use a drill of some sort. The drill and drill bit (cutting tool) that you choose to use will depend on the material that you are drilling into, its thickness and the size of the hole that you want.

■ STARTING OFF

Before you drill the hole you will need to mark out carefully where it is to go. If the material is hard or slippery you will also need to centre-punch the exact point where the hole is to be drilled, (Fig. 1). You simply put the point of the punch in position and give the punch a sharp tap. The small dent produced marks the centre of the hole and prevents the drill from skidding and scratching the surface.

■ USING A HAND DRILL

You can use this for making small holes in plastic, wood and metal. The three-jaw chuck on the drill holds the drill bit, usually a twist bit. You use a *chuck key* to tighten and release the drill bit from the chuck, (Fig. 2). It is important that the material which you are drilling is held firmly in a vice or by a G clamp, (Fig. 3). In this way you will be able to use both hands for operating and guiding the drill. If you are drilling right through the material it is important to have a piece of scrap wood behind the work piece. This stops the material splitting or tearing. If the material is thin and likely to break under pressure it is important to support it with scrap material.

■ USING A MACHINE DRILL

You can use a machine drill with a twist bit for making small holes in wood, metal and plastic. The machine makes it easier, and you can use a chuck key to tighten and release the drill bits. It is very important to check that the drill is located centrally in the chuck and that you have removed the chuck key before switching on. You must clamp the workpiece firmly into position on the drill table. For regular-shaped metal sections you can do this easily with a *machine vice*, (Fig. 4). The drill bit is simply pushed into the workpiece by pulling on the handle at the side of the machine. You can adjust how far through the material the drill goes by using the depth stop. Your teacher will show you how to do this and how to make sure that the drill speed is correct for the material you are drilling. You must wear goggles when using a machine drill and follow your teacher's instructions.

▷ Figure 1
Centre punching

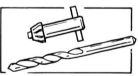
△ Figure 2
Chuck key and twist drill

△ Figure 3
Using a hand drill

Figure 4 *Using a pillar drill* △
Figure 5 *Holding work in a machine vice* ▷

■ USING A HOLE SAW

You use a hole saw for drilling large holes in wood and plastic. There is a range of sizes. It must be used in a machine drill. When you have drilled a hole you are left with a disc of wood which can be used for other parts of your design, e.g. wheels. You must clamp the workpiece firmly as shown and use scrap wood beneath the workpiece to protect the drill table.

■ USING FLAT BITS

You use flat bits for making clean-sided holes in wood. They must be used in a machine drill. Scrap wood is used to protect the drill table, and the workpiece must be firmly clamped. You can stop the wood from splitting on the side through which the hole breaks by following this method. Drill through the wood until the point is just visible from the underside. Then turn the work over and use the small hole made by the point to locate the drill bit and drill through from the other side.

■ USING A COUNTERSINK BIT

Countersink bits are used to widen the top of a drill hole so that a screw or bolt head will fit flush with the surface instead of sticking up. You can use these bits with both hand and machine drills. A deburring tool is similar to a countersink bit. It is used in a hand drill to remove any ragged edges inside holes drilled in sheet metal.

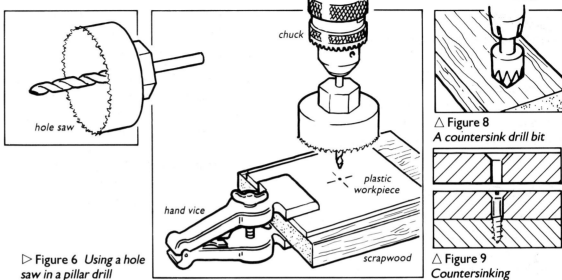

▷ Figure 6 *Using a hole saw in a pillar drill*

△ Figure 8
A countersink drill bit

△ Figure 9
Countersinking

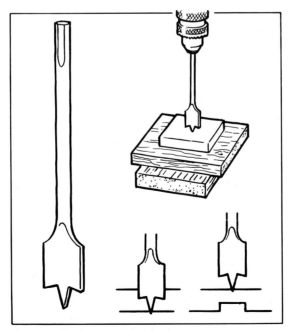

△ Figure 7 *Drilling with a flat bit*

Practical checklist

1. Have I marked where I want to drill?
2. Do I need to centre-punch?
3. What sort of drill bit do I need?
4. Do I need to use a hand drill or a machine drill?
5. How will I hold the workpiece?
6. Do I need to support the workpiece?

ACTIVITIES

Use flow charts to show how you would tackle the drilling that is required in the following projects:

■ mechanical toy (page 18);
■ moisture sensor (page 26);
■ model windmill (page 30).

Forming

Changing a flat piece of material into a 3D shape is called *forming*. Different methods of forming are used with different materials. All methods use pressure, and some use heat as well. For example, copper and aluminium can be formed cold simply by bending or hammering them into shape, providing they have been *annealed* first. Annealing is defined as heating and then cooling. Steel is easier to form when it is red hot *but you must follow very strict safety precautions* which your teacher will explain.

Thermoplastics like polystyrene and acrylic soften at quite low temperatures so it is easy for you to use heat and pressure to form them into complex shapes. Wood is difficult to form into shapes. It is only easy to bend when it is in very thin sheets called *veneers*. These can be bent into a required shape, clamped into that shape and then glued together. The resulting piece is strong but the process takes a long time.

■ BENDING METAL

Sheet metal can be bent into shape using folding bars. It is important to mark the work clearly so that you know exactly where you are going to make the bends. It is also important to decide on the best order to make the bends. You then position the work carefully in the folding bars and grip them in a vice. You make the bend by tapping with a wooden mallet, (Fig. 1).

You can bend metal strip and thin rod into quite complex shapes using a bending jig, (Fig. 2). You place metal pins in the holes to get the profile you want. You can then bend the metal strip around the pins. This method is very useful if you need several pieces the same shape.

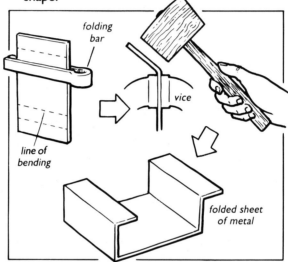

Figure 1 *Using folding bars*

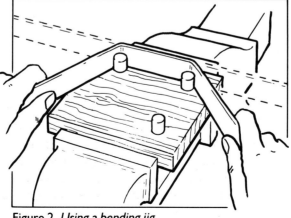

Figure 2 *Using a bending jig*

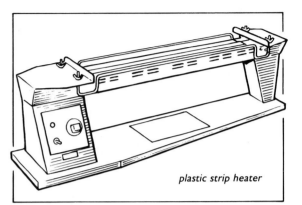

plastic strip heater

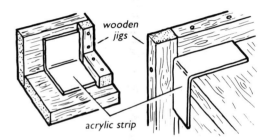

Figure 3 *Strip heating*

■ BENDING PLASTIC

You can bend plastic by using a strip heater, (Fig. 3). As with metal, you need to mark out where the bends will be and decide the best order to work in. You use the strip heater to heat along the line where you want to make a bend. It is important to heat the plastic enough to make it soft but not so much that it starts to bubble. You will need to watch carefully and heat the plastic from both sides. You can then bend the plastic into shape along the 'soft' line. As it cools the plastic sets hard. You can use a wooden former to help get exactly the angle of bend you want.

■ FORMING PLASTIC

You can use *plug and yoke moulding* to make simple shell forms from plastic sheet, (Fig. 4). You make the plastic soft and floppy by heating it in an oven. It is important not to overheat it. You place the floppy plastic sheet between the two halves of the plug and yoke and quickly clamp them tightly together using a vice or G clamp. You will need to wear heatproof gloves for this. As the plastic cools it will set hard into the shape of the former. When it is cool you can release your new shape. You will need to take care in making the former – the plug must fit inside the yoke but leave just enough room for the plastic sheet. The former is usually made from plywood or MDF. These are readily available in sheet form and are easy to work.

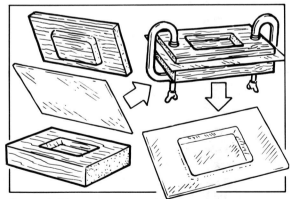

Figure 4 *Plug and yoke moulding (press-forming)*

You can use *vacuum-forming* to make more complex shell forms from plastic sheet, (Fig. 5). You heat the plastic to make it soft and floppy and then use a vacuum to suck the soft plastic over a wooden former. Both the heater and the vacuum pump are contained in the same machine called a vacuum former. You must take great care in making the wooden former. The slightest imperfection on the surface is transferred to the plastic. It is also very important for your former to have slightly sloping sides. This allows the plastic to come away easily from the former once it has set hard.

Figure 5 *Vacuum-forming to produce complex shell forms*

■ FORMING METAL

You can form metal into a hollow shape by *dishing*, (Fig. 6). You start with a flat metal shape. You must make sure that there are no sharp edges. You place the metal on a sandbag and hit it with a bossing mallet. Starting from the centre, you work outwards in increasing circles. The metal soon becomes dish shaped. After a while the metal will become more difficult to shape. This is called *work hardening*. You can make it soft again by annealing – heating and then cooling. Once you have the shape that you want you can get a good finish on the metal by *planishing* (Fig. 7). You place the dish over a metal stake and tap carefully with a hammer starting at the centre and working outwards. This will also 'work harden' the dish.

simple former

air holes

wooden former

formed plastic ready for trimming

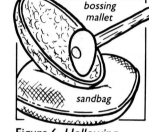

bossing mallet

sandbag

Figure 6 *Hollowing*

planishing hammer

stake

Figure 7 *Planishing*

ACTIVITIES

Look at each of the projects listed below and describe the forming process that you could use to make the solution:

- maze game (page 6);
- moisture sensor (page 26);
- body adornment (page 10).

Assembling

Before you join two pieces of material together you will need to think about these questions.

- Is the join temporary or permanent? Sometimes things need to be taken to pieces for maintenance or repair.
- Is the join rigid or flexible? Parts often need to be movable but still attached to one another.
- Which materials are to be joined? Adhesives that work for wood won't always work for metal or plastic.
- How strong must the join be? Some joining methods are much stronger than others but they take more time.
- How do you want the finished join to look? Some joining methods look much more attractive than others.

When you have answered these questions you will be able to compare your requirements with the joining methods available and make a sensible choice.

JOINING WOOD

■ USING GLUE

The simplest way to join two pieces of wood together in a way that is both permanent and rigid is to use wood glue. PVA glue comes ready-mixed, dries within one hour but is not

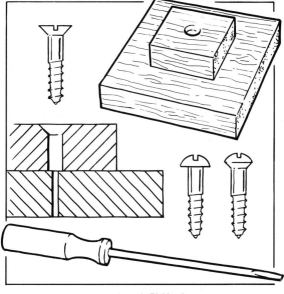

Figure 1 *Joining wood with PVA glue*

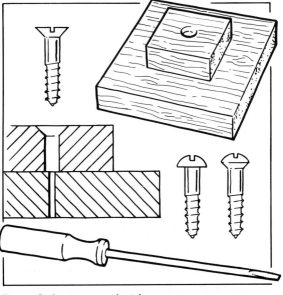

Figure 2 *Joining wood with screws*

waterproof. Cascamite comes as a powder which is mixed with water. It takes up to six hours to dry but forms a stronger, waterproof join. In both cases you need to hold the pieces of wood together while the glue is drying. You can do this by pinning them together or by using a G clamp, (Fig. 1).

■ USING WOOD SCREWS

If you want a temporary, rigid join then you will need to *screw* the pieces together. Depending on the final appearance you want you may use countersunk, raised-head or round-head wood screws. For the best results you need to drill both pilot and clearance holes, (see Fig. 2).

JOINING PLASTIC

■ USING ADHESIVES

If you want to make a permanent, rigid join between two pieces of plastic then you must use the correct adhesive. Most of these adhesives give off harmful fumes so you should take special care to work in a well ventilated area. It is important to find the right glue for the plastic you are using. The wrong one could 'eat' into your plastic. You will need to follow the instructions carefully, (Fig. 3).

■ USING SELF-TAPPING SCREWS

The easiest way to make a temporary, rigid join is to use a self-tapping screw. As plastic has no grain you cannot use wood screws.

Self-tapping screws are designed to cut a thread in the soft plastic so that the screw cannot be pulled out. You need to drill both clearance and pilot holes as shown in Fig. 5. Several styles of screw head are available: countersunk, raised-head, round-head and cheese-head.

JOINING METAL

■ USING NUTS AND BOLTS

You can make a temporary, rigid join easily using a nut and screw. You need to drill a clearance hole in both pieces. If the pieces are to be held tightly together you need to use a nut and bolt. You should use a plain washer to protect the surface of the metal and a spring washer to stop the nut and bolt from working loose, (Fig. 4).

■ TAPPING THREADS

You cannot use nuts and bolts if you can only get to one side of the material once it has been assembled. Self-tapping screws can be used on soft metals but not steel. You can make a temporary, rigid join for steel pieces by drilling a hole in one piece and tapping a thread in this hole. You use a special tapping tool that has hardened cutting edges, as shown in Fig. 6. The thread cut into the sides of the hole will take a particular size screw. Drilling a clearance hole in the other piece of steel allows the screw to pass through into the threaded hole.

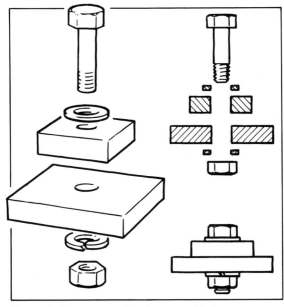

Figure 3 *Joining acrylic with tensol cement*

Figure 4 *Joining metal with nuts and bolts*

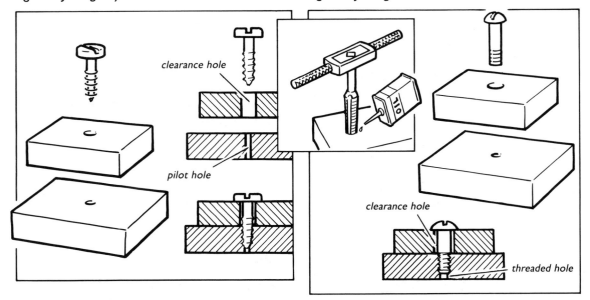

Figure 5 *Using self-tapping screws to join acrylic*

Figure 6 *Joining metal by tapping a thread*

If you want to make a permanent, rigid join between metals then you should use *solder*. You can use it for all metals except aluminium. The three types of solder that you will find in school are all used in a similar way. The solder acts just like a glue. It sticks to each piece of metal and so holds them together. You make the solder 'sticky' by melting it. As it cools down it becomes a solid but it still 'sticks' to the pieces of metal.

The metal must be very clean for the solder to stick to it. You clean the parts of the metal where you want the solder to go by using a flux. To begin with the pieces of metal to be joined must be clean and grease free. There must be a good fit between the parts to be joined so there are no gaps where they touch. Then you carefully apply the flux just where you want the solder to go. You then heat the metal pieces using a blow torch. *Be very careful*. The flux bubbles and cleans the metal.

When both pieces of metal are glowing red hot you touch the solder onto the parts where the join is to be made. It should flow freely over the parts cleaned by the flux. You then let the metal pieces cool down and the join is made. The joined pieces may be cooled using water once the solder has gone solid. Be careful because the metal will still be very hot.

■ SOFT SOLDERING

You can use soft solder to join copper and brass. It is used in plumbing. The flux looks like grease. The solder melts at a low temperature 220°C. The join is not very strong.

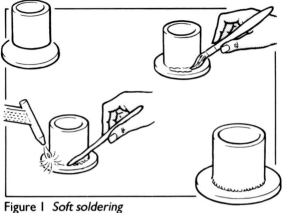

Figure 1 *Soft soldering*

Figure 2 *Silver soldering*

■ SILVER SOLDERING

Silver solders give stronger joins than soft solders. The flux is a white powder that you mix with water to form a paste. Silver solders melt from 700°C to 800°C. They are used for silver and gold as well as copper and brass.

■ HARD SOLDERING

This is sometimes called *brazing*. You can use it to join steel. The joints are very strong. The flux is a pink powder that you mix with water. Hard solder melts at 960°C.

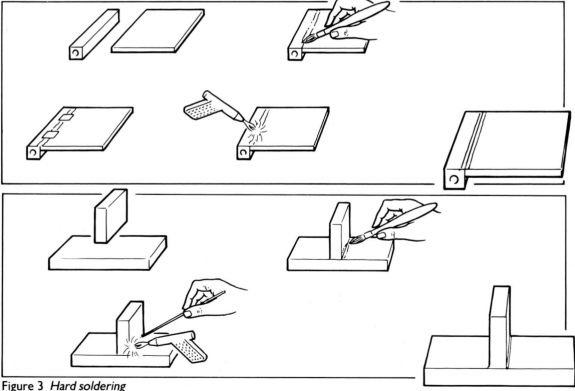

Figure 3 *Hard soldering*

FRAMEWORKS

■ FROM WOODEN STRIP

You can join thin wooden strips together to form a framework by gluing card triangles across the joins, (Fig. 4). PVA is a suitable glue and you can use staples to hold the join together while the glue dries. If you are in a hurry your teacher might let you use a glue gun, (Fig. 5). The hot glue 'dries' very quickly. As frameworks like this can be made quickly they are very useful for mock-ups and for trying out ideas. You can make the joins much stronger by using thin plywood instead of card.

■ STRONGER FRAMES

For a very strong frame you have to use thicker wood and cut a halving joint (Fig. 6). This takes a lot longer to make. You mark out both pieces of wood and then carefully cut away the parts that are not needed. The two pieces should fit together without any gaps. If you want a permanent join, you glue the two pieces together. If you want a temporary join, use wood screws.

■ FROM METAL TUBE

Square tube is easier to join than round tube. If you need a frame that can be taken to pieces you can use triangular metal plates and bolt them to the tube as shown in Fig. 7. You must drill the holes accurately if the bolts are to pass straight through the plates and the tube.

Figure 4 *Wooden strip used to make a frame by using card corners*

Figure 5 *Glue guns make gluing quick and easy*

Figure 6 *Stronger frames can be jointed by a halving joint*

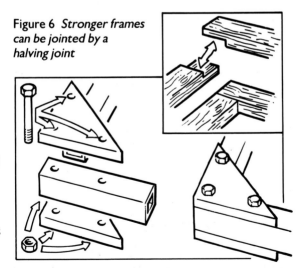

Figure 7 *Assembling a frame from square section tube*

Figure 8 *Using pop rivets to make a permanent frame*

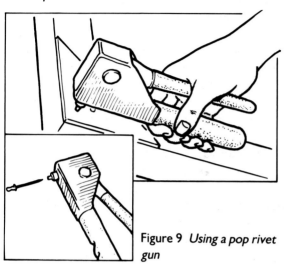

Figure 9 *Using a pop rivet gun*

■ USING POP RIVETS

If the frame does not need to be taken to pieces you can use pop rivets, (Fig. 8). Once the holes have been drilled you can quickly get the rivets in place with the rivet gun. You may need help to squeeze it shut. You can use pop riveting where you cannot use nuts and bolts. The rivets go in from one side only and you don't need to be able to get to the other side.

■ BRAZING

You can join steel tube by *brazing*. This gives a very strong frame that will not come to pieces. You braze the pieces of steel together as described on page 116. This is not easy so you should be sure there is no other way to make the frame you want.

■ FROM PLASTIC TUBE

You can join plastic tubes together by using the correct adhesive. The joins are not very strong. Gluing triangular corner plates made from the same plastic over the joins improves the strength, (Fig. 1). The best way to make plastic tube frames is to use special joining pieces which fit into the ends of the tubes to be joined together. If a permanent join is required these pieces can be glued into place, (Fig. 2). This method allows you to model structures very quickly.

▽ Figure 1 *Using plastic tube to make a framework by gluing*

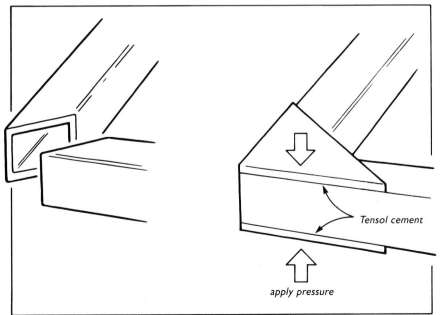

Tensol cement

apply pressure

△ Figure 2
A plastic frame assembled with joining pieces

BOXES

Boxes are small containers. You can make a box by joining flat pieces of wood, or plastic, edge to edge. Three simple ways of doing this are shown in Fig. 3. In each case you must prepare the starting materials very carefully. Check that the edges are straight and mark out each piece so that you can cut it out accurately. You may be able to use a sanding wheel to get the edges of each piece smooth so that the sides fit together well. If you are using wood you can join the sides together with both pins and glue. The pins hold the sides together while the glue dries. If you are using plastic you have to clamp the sides together as you cannot use pins. The top and bottom pieces can be joined to the sides and then the lid can be sawn off as shown in Fig. 4.

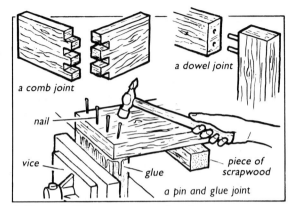

a comb joint

a dowel joint

nail

vice

glue

piece of scrapwood

a pin and glue joint

△ Figure 3 *Three ways to make a box*

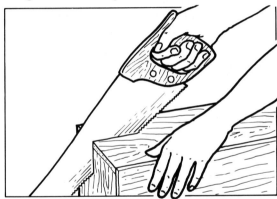

△ Figure 4 *This way the lid has to fit!*

ACTIVITIES

Look at the projects listed below and note down the ways of assembly that have been used in each:

- maze game (page 6);
- body adornment (page 10);
- model movers (page 14);
- mechanical toy (page 18);
- moisture sensor (page 26);
- windmill (page 30).

FLEXIBLE JOINTS

■ PIN JOINTS

You will find pin joints very useful when you design simple lever mechanisms. The simplest is a paper fastener. It slips through the holes in two thin pieces of material, e.g. paper, card or lolly stick. The head stops it going right through and the ends can be bent over to stop it coming out, (Fig. 5).

The paper fastener does not give a very strong pin joint. It will break with heavy use so it is best used for modelling. You can make a stronger pin joint by using wooden dowel for the pin, and plastic tube to stop the pin coming out. The holes in the material being joined should give a sliding fit for the dowel. The plastic tube must fit tightly on the dowel. Thicker materials can be pin-jointed using dowel pins. The joint can be taken to pieces by removing the plastic tube, (Fig. 6).

Fig. 7 shows how you use a screw and lock nut with washers to make a very strong pin joint. This is easy to take to pieces.

■ HINGE JOINTS

You can make simple hinge joints by using fabric hinges, (Fig. 8). Heavy cloth and canvas are easy to use and you can staple them to wood or glue them to metal or plastic with an epoxy adhesive. Using leather gives you a stronger hinge.

There is a wide variety of metal hinges. Small box hinges look attractive but are difficult to fit really well, (Fig. 9). The piano hinge is easier to fit because the chiselling out is not quite so difficult, (Fig. 10). Both sorts of hinges are attached to wood with small screws. You can join them to plastic or metal sheet using pop rivets or epoxy adhesive. If the plastic is thick enough you can use self-tapping screws.

Corrugated plastic sheet can be turned into a flexible material which is useful for hinges, (Fig. 11). You must be careful to cut through just one layer of plastic. You staple the hinge to wood, rivet it to metal or glue it to other plastics with epoxy adhesive.

▽ Figure 5 *This pin joint is useful in models*

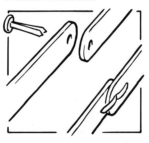

△ Figure 6 *A pin joint using dowel and plastic tube*

▽ Figure 7 *A very strong pin joint*

△ Figure 8 *A fabric hinge – simple but effective*

△ Figure 9 *A small box hinge – attractive but difficult to fit*

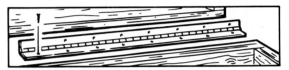

△ Figure 10 *Piano hinge*

◁Figure 11 *Using corrugated plastic sheet for a hinge*

ACTIVITIES

Look at the projects listed and note where flexible joints are required. In each case, suggest how they might be achieved:

- maze game (page 6);
- model movers (page 14);
- problems with play (page 40);
- wind-powered pump (page 52);
- lifebelt thrower (page 51);
- spinning games (page 47);
- puppet theatre (page 49).

Mechanical systems

FREE WHEELS ON FIXED AXLES

Your design may need a wheel to spin freely on a fixed axle. To make this you will need to drill a clearance hole in the wheel for the wheel to spin freely. You must find a way to stop the wheel coming off the axle. A simple method is to use tight-fitting plastic tubing, (Fig. 1). You can also use this tubing to act as a spacer to prevent the wheel moving along the axle and rubbing against the framework. If the gap between the wheel and the framework is small you can use metal washers.

FIXED WHEELS

Sometimes your design will need a wheel fixed to an axle so that when the axle turns the wheel turns as well. It is easiest to do this by drilling a hole that is a tight fit for the axle. The axle can then be tapped into the hole in the wheel, (Fig. 2). This does make the wheel difficult to change.

▽ Figure 1 *Free wheel on a fixed axle*

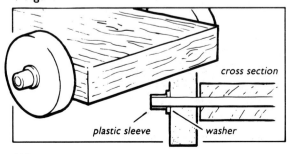

cross section

plastic sleeve   washer

FIXED CAMS

Your design may need a cam fixed onto an axle at a particular alignment. You could use a simple tight fit but the cam might slip. A better way is to use a tight fit plus a key way as shown in Fig. 3. You can cut the key way in both the axle and the cam with a narrow file. You can make the key from hardboard. With this method you can easily change cams.

▽ Figure 2 *Fitting a fixed wheel onto an axle*

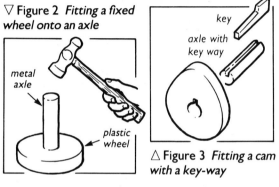

metal axle

plastic wheel

key

axle with key way

△ Figure 3 *Fitting a cam with a key-way*

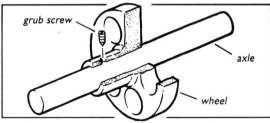

grub screw

axle

wheel

△ Figure 4 *Fitting a wheel with a grub screw*

USING GRUB SCREWS

It is difficult to cut key ways into narrow metal axles so it is often easier to buy wheels that can be fixed onto axles using grub screws. This is particularly useful for gear wheels, (Fig. 4).

USING BEARINGS

If the axle as well as the wheel has to turn then it is important to design the parts that support the axle so that there is as little friction as possible. For wooden axles supported in wood, talcum powder or candle wax will help. Steel axles often 'bind' in wood. You cannot use oil as this soaks into the wood. You can use nylon inserts or ball races, (Fig. 5).

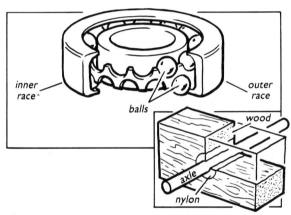

inner race

balls

outer race

wood

axle

nylon

△ Figure 5 *You can use bearings or bushes to support axles*

ACTIVITIES

Look at the projects listed and note where mechanical systems have been designed, and the fixing arrangement that has been used:

- model movers (page 14);
- mechanical toy (page 18);
- windmill (page 30);
- spinning games (page 47).

Electrical assembly

MODELLING CIRCUITS

You often need to check that the circuit you have designed does what you want it to. It is important that you do this in a way that is quick and easy before you spend a lot of time producing the finished circuit. This modelling does not involve soldering.

△ Figure 6 *You can model simple circuits like this*

For simple circuits an easy way is to use *pin board* and drawing pins to join the components together as shown in Fig. 6. For more complex circuits you can use *base boards* and components mounted in special boxes that clip together. This allows for very rapid assembly, (see Fig. 7).

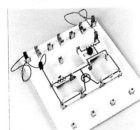

▷ Figure 7
You can use this for rapid circuit modelling

For circuits that use chips you can use *protoboard*. With this you plug in chips and other components so that they are joined up according to your circuit diagram, (see Fig. 8).

△ Figure 8 *This way you can use microchips*

SOLDERING CIRCUITS

There are two ways of soldering circuits. Each has advantages and disadvantages.

■ MATRIX BOARD

This board contains lots of pre-drilled holes. You can push small pins in the holes and then solder components and connecting wire to them. The advantage of this method is that the circuit produced looks just like the circuit diagram. This makes fault-finding easy. The disadvantages are that it is not suitable for use with chips, and the circuits take up more room.

▽ Figure 9 *Circuit mounted on matrix board*

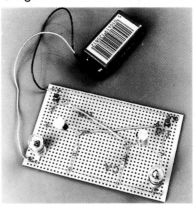

■ PRINTED CIRCUIT BOARDS (PCBs)

Pcbs are the best way to produce a soldered circuit. They begin as a copper-coated board and parts of the copper are etched away to leave a series of connecting points for the circuit required. Pcbs can be used with chips and single components. The advantages are that layout can be designed to take up minimum space and this is the method used in industry. The disadvantage is that pcbs take a long time to produce.

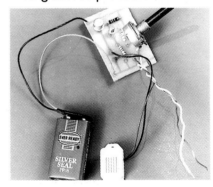

△ Figure 10 *Circuit mounted on a pcb*

HOW TO MAKE A PRINTED CIRCUIT BOARD

HOW TO SOLDER

Stage 1
Draw out the circuit diagram.

Stage 2
Plan the layout diagram of the circuit on tracing paper. Take care to make sure that the components can reach.

Stage 3
Turn the tracing paper over and place onto the copper-clad board. Rub firmly to transfer the layout onto the board.

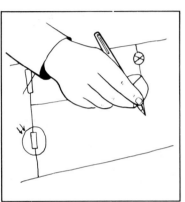

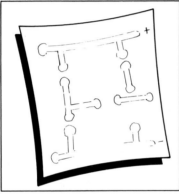

Stage 4
Remove the tracing paper and go over the layout on the copper with an etch resist pen. Leave a small hole uncovered at the centre of each connection.

Stage 5
Place the pcb in the etch tank to remove the unwanted copper. This takes 10 – 15 minutes. Wash the etched board and clean the copper tracks gently with wire wool.

Stage 6
Dry the board and drill holes in the circuit board to take the components.

You use an electrical soldering iron to solder, (Fig. 1). When it is switched on the tip gets very hot so be careful *not* to touch it or put it on the supply cable. Use the tip of the iron to heat the parts to be joined together. You should apply solder only when they are hot. Electrical solder comes on reels and looks like thick wire, (Fig. 1). It contains a flux which helps the solder to flow over the parts to be joined. Once the parts have been heated, just touch the solder onto the joint. Make sure it flows over the joint but use the solder sparingly, (Fig. 1). Then remove the solder and the soldering iron and let the joint cool so that the solder sets hard. If the solder looks 'blobby' then you probably did not heat the parts enough. This is called a 'dry' joint and it will not conduct electricity.

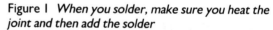

Figure 1 *When you solder, make sure you heat the joint and then add the solder*

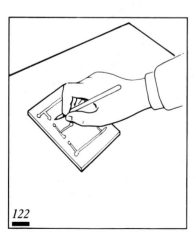

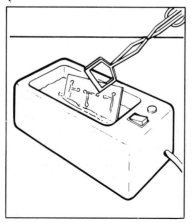

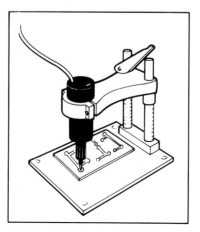

Shaping

You often need to shape a piece of material. This is usually done by removing waste material so that you are left with the shape that you want. Your choice of tools will depend on the material you are shaping, how much waste material is to be removed and the shape that you require. Whichever tool you choose, you will need to make sure that the material is firmly held, in a vice or by a G clamp.

SHAPING METAL AND PLASTIC

■ CHOOSING FILES

Files come in five shapes – square, triangular, flat, half-round and round (see Fig. 2). You choose the shape which is best for the shape you want to make. e.g. for an inside curve use a half-round. Each of these shapes is available in a range of sizes from large, (20 mm or so across), to small needle files. They come in a range of roughness or 'cuts'. The very rough ones have large teeth for removing large amounts of material quickly. The smooth ones with small teeth are used to 'finish off' a shape before polishing.

■ USING FILES

Cross filing is used to remove waste quickly by filing down to a line. You do this by holding both ends of the file as shown in Fig. 3 and pushing the file to and fro across the surface of the material.

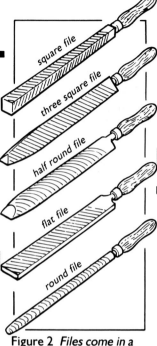

Figure 2 *Files come in a range of shapes and sizes*

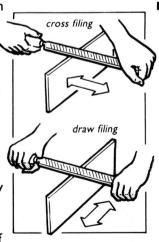

Figure 3 *Two ways to file*

Draw filing is used to give a smooth shiny finish. You use a file with small teeth, hold it as shown in Fig. 3 and push the file to and fro along the length of the material. You can use small files to make slots from drill holes placed close together.

SHAPING WOOD

■ USING SURFORMS

A surform is a special tool to shape wood. Surforms come in a range of sizes with a variety of handles. They work like cheese graters. The cutting blades can be changed and are available in three forms: flat, half-round and round (Fig. 4). You use them like a file but they cut only on the *forward* stroke. You can also use a rasp to shape wood. This is a large file with coarse teeth.

■ USING CHISELS

You use chisels to cut away small amounts of waste wood. They are very useful for cutting out joints. They are very sharp and must be used with great care. Make sure that you always have *both* hands *behind* the cutting edge. Then, if the chisel slips, there is no danger of you cutting yourself. You cut with a chisel by pushing it into the wood with your hand or by tapping it with a mallet (Fig. 5). When cutting out a piece between two saw cuts, it is important to work from *both* sides as shown to stop the wood splitting. Chisels can be used to cut away the wood between drill holes to produce slots.

Figure 4 *You can use these to shape wood*

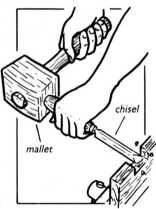

Figure 5 *Remember to keep both hands behind the cutting edge*

Finishing

You apply a *finish* to a material to protect it from the environment and to enhance its appearance. Before you can do this the surface of the material must be made as smooth as possible. The exact method you use will depend on the material you are smoothing but all methods involve using abrasive papers. You always start with the roughest paper and work through the various grades until you are using the finest. Each paper removes the scratches made by the one before so, when you have finished, the scratches remaining are so small that the material feels completely smooth.

SMOOTHING WOOD

You use glasspaper to smooth wood. For flat surfaces, you wrap this around a wood or cork block. This ensures a flat surface. It is important to move the glasspaper along the direction of the grain. For curved surfaces, you can wrap the glasspaper around dowel rod.

SMOOTHING PLASTIC

It is only the edges of the plastic that you will need to finish as the sides are protected by paper covering. If this comes off it is important to replace it. Smooth the edges by draw filing and then use silicon carbide abrasive paper. You should dip the paper in water before using and re-wet it as it starts to dry out.

Figure 1 *Smoothing wood*

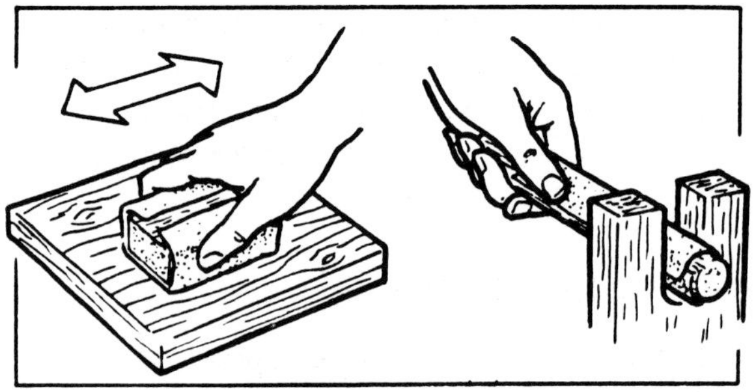

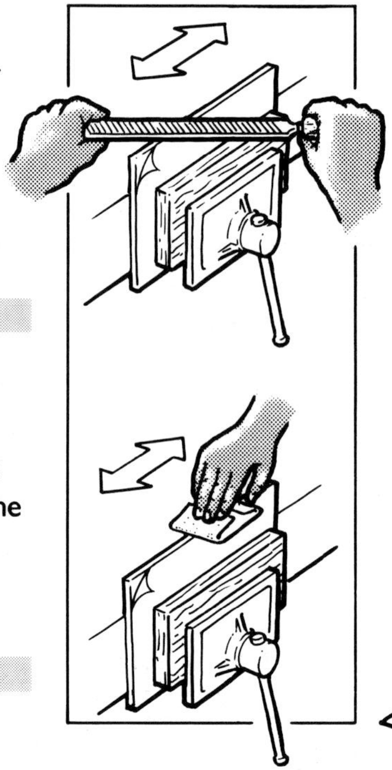

Figure 2
Smoothing plastic

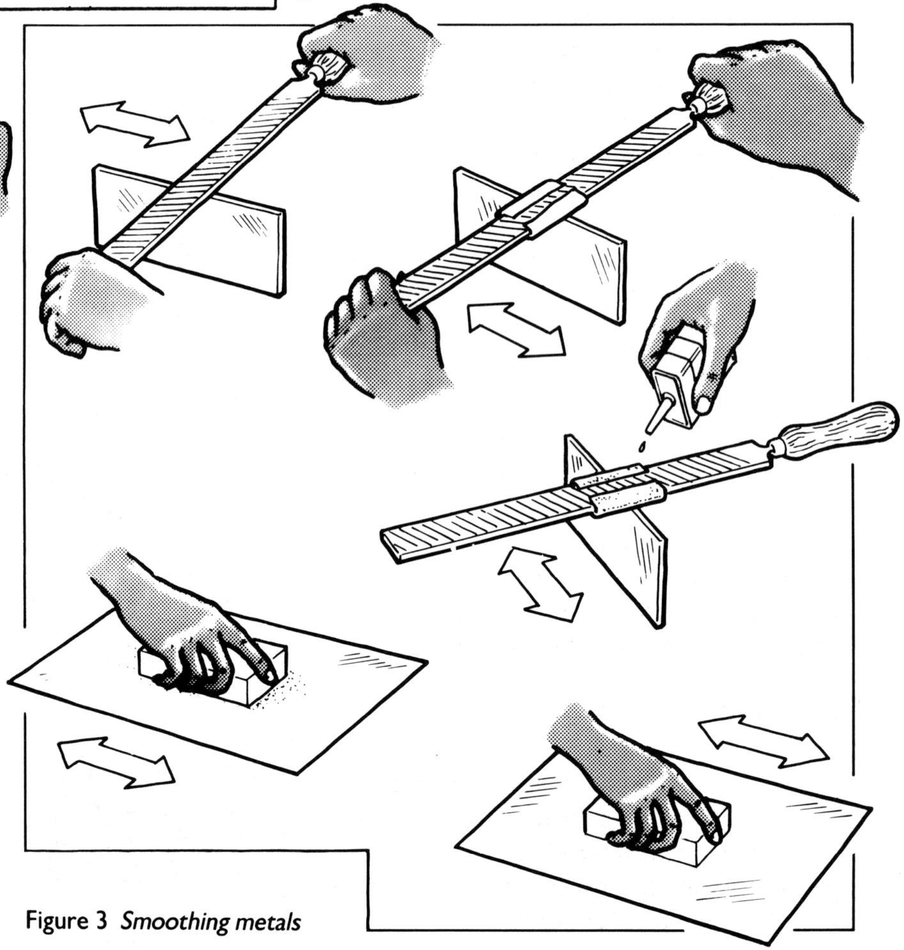

SMOOTHING METAL

As with plastic you draw file the edges first. Then you use emery cloth. To ensure a flat surface wrap the cloth around a file. Use oil with the fine grade emery cloth to get a smooth finish with steel. For aluminium or brass you use pumice powder and water of Ayr stone to get a really good finish.

Figure 3 *Smoothing metals*

CHOOSING FINISHES

The finish you choose to apply to a material will depend on the material, the environment it has to resist, and the final appearance you want. Wood swells if it gets too damp and shrinks if it gets too dry. So finishes for wood seal the surface to prevent water getting in or out. Small animals and fungus eat wood so, if it is to be used outside, it is treated with a preservative to prevent this. Steel rusts so is best protected by a layer of paint, grease or oil. Non-ferrous metals like copper and brass do not rust but they do tarnish. You can prevent this by coating them with a clear lacquer. Without this they require regular polishing.

Most plastics do not need a finish as they do not react to the environment like wood and metal.

■ FINISHING WOOD

You can use a wood stain to change the colour of wood and let the grain pattern show through. Note that this does not protect the wood, it simply changes the colour. You apply the stain with a cotton wool pad, being careful to spread the colour evenly. To protect wood you must coat it with a polyurethane varnish. This can go onto bare or stained wood. Make sure that any stain has dried thoroughly before applying varnish.

You brush a thin coat of the varnish onto the wood. Brush from the centre to the outside. Leave the work to dry and then rub down gently with very fine glasspaper. Give a further coat of varnish and allow to dry.

You apply paint in a similar way. Of course you cannot see the grain through paint. Bare wood needs a coat of primer paint. When this is dry it is rubbed down and you apply a coat of undercoat. This is rubbed down when dry and then you apply a top coat.

■ FINISHING PLASTIC

To finish the edge of a piece of plastic you simply rub it hard with a clean cloth and metal polish.

■ FINISHING METAL

You can make all metals shine by polishing them on a buffing wheel. There are different types of polishing compound for different metals. Always wear safety goggles when using a buffing wheel and never buff small pieces.

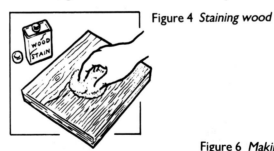

Figure 4 *Staining wood*

Figure 5 *Applying varnish*

Figure 6 *Making the plastic shine*

Figure 7 *Buffing*　　　　Figure 8 *Dip coating*

■ PLASTIC DIP COATING

You can cover a piece of metal with a thin layer of plastic by dip coating. The plastic will protect the metal from air and moisture. It will also make the metal more comfortable to hold and attractive. To begin with make sure that the metal is clean and free from oil and grease. Then, holding the metal in a pair of tongs, heat it slowly and evenly up to 160°C. You then dip the hot metal into a fluidising tank filled with plastic powder for 10 – 15 seconds. Some of the plastic power melts and sticks to the metal covering it with a thin plastic coating. Leave the coated piece to cool for at least 15 minutes.

ACTIVITIES

Draw a flow chart to show the finishing necessary in the following projects:

maze game (page 6);
body adornment (page 10);
mechanical toy (page 18);
moisture sensor (page 26).

Project evaluation

Your Name	Group	Teacher's Name	Day and Session	Start Date	Finish Date

THE CHALLENGE

	pupil / teacher YES	pupil / teacher NO	

FINDING OUT

Did I do this?	Did I find out enough?				Comments

THINKING UP IDEAS

Did I do this?	Did I think up several ideas?				Comments

DEVELOPING IDEAS

Did I do this?	Did I consider – different ways of working? – different materials? – different construction techniques?				Comments

MODELLING THE BEST IDEA

Did I do this?	Did my model help me understand and detail my design?				Comments

PRESENTING THE BEST IDEA

Did I do this?	Did my presentation show my design clearly to other people?				Comments

MAKING IT

Did I do this?	Did I use the tools/equipment – safely? – correctly?				Comments

TESTING IT

Did I do this?	Did the test help me see where improvements could be made?				Comments

Index

abrafile 109
adhesives 114, 115
advertising 39, 44
alternative energy 87
anemometer 53
annealing 112, 113
anthropometrics 78
assembling 114–119
axles 120

base leg 103
batteries 84, 100
beams 90
belt drive 93
bearings 120
bending 112
bicycle 58, 92
blister packs 45
body adornment 10–13
boxes 118
bulbs 100, 101

cams 19, 94
capacitors 114
car games 6–9
cascamite 114
chain drive 92
chisels 123
chuck key 110
circuit diagram 100
circuits
    electric organ 105
    flashing light 104
    monostable 105
    noise making 104
    parallel 101
    series 101
    water sensing 27, 103
collector leg 103
columns 90
compressed air 96
compression 90
computer control 107
computers 106–107
computer simulation 107
conductivity 80
container 24, 36, 56, 57, 118
corrosion 80
countersink bit 111
crank 52, 95

crank slider 95
crating 65
cross sections 67
cutting 109

databases 107
density 80
designing mechanisms 95
designing pneumatic toys 96
design strip 4
detail drawing 67
developing ideas 7, 11, 15, 19,
    27, 32, 33
developments 17, 63
dimensioning 73
dip coating 125
dishing 113
dividers 108
drill
    hand 92, 110
    machine 110
    pillar 110
drive shaft 19

effort 94
electrical assembly 121
electricity and
    electronics 100–105
ellipses 68
emitter leg 103
end elevation 72
energy 84–89
enlarging 66
erasers 60
ergonomics 78
evaluating 126
exploded views 69

files 123
finding out 6, 10, 14, 18, 22, 26
fine line markers 60
finishing 125
flat bits 110
flux 116
folding bars 112
food
    convenience 56, 57
    health 37
    takeaway 56, 57
forces 90

forecourts 54
form 63
forming
    plug and yoke 113
    press 113
    vacuum 9, 28, 113
fossil fuel 86
frameworks 9, 117
freehand drawing 61
friction 85
front elevation 72

games
    maze 6
    fantasy 47
G–clamp 109
gears 94
    bevelled gears 92
    compound gears 94
ghosting 67
glue 114
grids 64
grippers 99
grub screw 120

hand size 79
hidden detail 67, 73
hinge joints 119
hole saw 111
hot air balloon 43
hydraulics 98

image processing 106
interview 6
integrated circuits 105
isometric view 68

joining 115

key ways 120
kites 22, 42

LDR (light dependent
    resistor) 53, 103
LED (light-emitting diode) 27,
    101
lettering 76
levers 94
library 6, 30
linkage 95

load 94
lubrication 85

machine vice 110
making 9, 13, 17, 21, 29
mallet 113, 123
marking out 108
materials 80–83
    for model making 71
    forms 82, 83
    properties 80
matrix board 121
mechanical systems 120
mechanical toy 18–21
mechanisms 92–95
model mover 14–17
modelling circuits 121
modelling ideas 8, 12, 16, 20,
    24, 28, 30
model making 70
moisture sensor 26–29, 103
motor
    electric 16, 102
    spring 84, 86
music makers 48, 104, 105

National Curriculum 3
nuclear energy 85
nuts and bolts 115

oblique view 64
odd leg calipers 108

packaging 24, 25, 44
paper 60
paper punch 92, 94
parts list 73
pencils 60
perspective 75
pin joints 119
planishing 113
plan view 72
Plasticine 12, 63
play 40
play ground 41
play structures 41
plug and yoke 113
pneumatics 96
pop-up cards 46
power 31, 88, 89

presentation 77
pressure 97
problems with play 40, 41
project evaluation sheet 127
promotion 38
publicity 38
pump 52
puppets 49, 97
puppet theatre 49
pva glue 114

reducing 66
resistor
    colour code 101
    fixed 101
    variable 101
rubber bands 84
rusting 80

saw
    abrafile 109
    coping saw 109
    hack 109
    hole 111
    mechanical 95
    tenon 109
sawing board 109
self-tapping screws 114
sensors 103
shape 62
shapes and sizes 78
shaping 123
shopfront 32, 33
shops 54
sketching 61
slider 95
sliding fit 92
smoothing 124
soldering
    electrical 121–123
    hard 116
    silver 116
    soft 116
spinning games 47
springs 84, 86
sprockets 92
steam engine 87
stiffness 80
storing energy 84
straight edge 108

strength 80
strip heater 112
structures 90
sunshine 51
supermarkets 54, 55
surforms 123
survival 34, 35, 50, 51
switches 100–103
    home-made 100
    membrane panel 102
    reed 102
    tilt 103
syringes 97, 98, 99

tabs 63
tapping threads 115
templates 108
tension 90
tensol cement 114, 115
testing 9, 13, 17, 21, 29, 30, 31
textures 74
thermistor 103
thinking up ideas 7, 11, 15, 19,
    27
tinsnips 109
transistor 27, 103
try square 108
tumble drier 93

untidy desk 36

vacuum cleaner 93
variation 78
vice 109

warnings 59
water probes 27, 103
weather 53
wheels 120
wind energy 52
windmill 30
wood screws 114
work 31, 88, 89
work hardening 113
working drawings 72
working properties 81